I0411453

Report Number: I333-034-2004

Systems Management Server 2003® Security Guide

Network Applications Team
of the
Systems and Network Attack Center

April 2005
Version 1.0

National Security Agency
ATTN: I33
9800 Savage Road
Ft. Meade, Maryland 20755-6704

Warnings

Do not attempt to implement any of the settings in this guide without first testing in a non-operational environment.

This document is only a guide, containing recommended security settings. It is not meant to replace well-structured policy or sound judgment. Furthermore, this guide does not address site-specific configuration issues. Care must be taken when implementing this guide to address local operational and policy concerns.

The security changes described in this document apply only to the Microsoft® Windows systems referenced herein and should not be applied to any other operating systems or applications.

THIS DOCUMENT IS PROVIDED "AS IS" AND ANY EXPRESS OR IMPLIED WARRANTIES, INCLUDING, BUT NOT LIMITED TO, THE IMPLIED WARRANTIES OF MERCHANTABILITY AND FITNESS FOR A PARTICULAR PURPOSE ARE EXPRESSLY DISCLAIMED. IN NO EVENT SHALL THE CONTRIBUTORS BE LIABLE FOR ANY DIRECT, INDIRECT, INCIDENTAL, SPECIAL, EXEMPLARY, OR CONSEQUENTIAL DAMAGES (INCLUDING, BUT NOT LIMITED TO, PROCUREMENT OF SUBSTITUTE GOODS OR SERVICES; LOSS OF USE, DATA, OR PROFITS; OR BUSINESS INTERRUPTION) HOWEVER CAUSED AND ON ANY THEORY OF LIABILITY, WHETHER IN CONTRACT, STRICT LIABILITY, OR TORT (INCLUDING NEGLIGENCE OR OTHERWISE) ARISING IN ANY WAY OUT OF THE USE OF THIS SOFTWARE, EVEN IF ADVISED OF THE POSSIBILITY OF SUCH DAMAGE.

See Microsoft's web site for the latest changes or modifications to the Windows operating systems and applications referenced herein.

UNCLASSIFIED

Acknowledgment

We thank the MITRE Corporation for its collaborative effort in the development of this guide. Working closely with our NSA representatives, the MITRE team—Joe Kusmiss (task leader) and Len LaPadula (task product manager)—building on an earlier MITRE guide to the Beta version of SMS 2003, generated most of the security recommendations in this guide and produced the first draft. Additional MITRE contributors to the earlier guide were Rosalie McQuaid and Ellen Laderman.

Trademark Information

Table of Contents

UNCLASSIFIED

UNCLASSIFIED

List of Figures

List of Tables

UNCLASSIFIED

Introduction

The purpose of this guide is to inform the reader about secure configuration and operation of Systems Management Server 2003® (SMS). This guide is based on the first release of SMS 2003, running on Windows Server 2003.

> NOTE: This guide does not address security issues for the Microsoft Windows Server 2003 operating system that are not specifically related to the Systems Management Server.

This guide is intended for individuals with basic knowledge of SMS and Windows operating systems, Windows Server 2003 and Windows XP® in particular, who are looking for guidance on how to make operation of SMS 2003 more secure. It may also benefit anyone involved with or interested in SMS 2003, other Enterprise Management systems, or network security.

The emphasis in this guide is on general security guidelines. It does not cover issues relevant to topologies and configurations, design questions such as site hierarchies and secondary Site Servers, and other large-scale design issues.

This document assumes that the reader who implements the security recommendations in this guide is a knowledgeable Windows Server 2003 administrator. A knowledgeable Windows Server 2003 administrator is defined as someone who can create and manage accounts and groups, understands how Windows Server 2003 performs access control, understands how to set account policies and security rights, and is familiar with how to set up auditing and how to read audit logs. This document does not provide step-by-step instructions on how to perform these basic Windows Server 2003 administrative functions—it is assumed that the reader is capable of implementing basic instructions regarding Windows Server 2003 administration.

Getting the Most from this Guide

> WARNING: The following list does not address site-specific issues. Test every setting or suggestion in this guide on a nonoperational network.

The following list contains suggestions to ensure successful use of this guide:

- ❑ Read the guide in its entirety. Note that some of the security recommendations are interdependent. Selectively implementing recommendations may cause unexpected results.
- ❑ Perform these preconfiguration recommendations:
    - ❑ Do a complete backup of your system before implementing any of the recommendations in this guide.
    - ❑ Ensure that the latest SMS service packs and hotfixes have been installed. For further information on critical SMS updates, see the Microsoft Systems Management Server home page (at http://www.microsoft.com/smserver/) and the Microsoft Knowledge Base (at http://support.microsoft.com/).
- ❑ Use security settings that are appropriate for your environment.

Important Notes about Operating System and Physical Security

Systems Management Server 2003 security is tightly coupled to the operating system. File permissions, registry settings, password usage, user rights, and other issues associated with Windows Server 2003 security have a direct impact on Systems Management Server security. The recommended source of information for how to securely configure Windows Server 2003 is the set of *NSA Windows 2000 Security Guides* and the Microsoft Windows Server 2003 Security Guide. [9] It is important to implement these guides on the Systems Management Server machines.

Systems Management Server 2003 has functional capabilities that can be used by an uninformed or malicious user to disrupt an enterprise's operation. Access to the computers on which these capabilities reside is a first significant step toward accessing these capabilities. That is, a user able to physically access the computer has a good chance of accessing the capabilities available on that computer. Thus, enterprise managers should carefully consider providing physical access protection for the SMS component servers.

About this Guide

This document consists of the following chapters:

Chapter 1 – Enterprise Management and Systems Management Server 2003 discusses basic ideas about Enterprise Management, outlining the functional areas that make up Enterprise Management and applying them to Enterprise Management Systems and Systems Management Server 2003 in particular. In addition, it presents a number of security recommendations for Enterprise Management Systems.

Chapter 2 – Architectural Considerations provides security recommendations for general deployment of SMS 2003 in a site hierarchy, introducing essential terms needed in discussing SMS and discussing the technologies that support SMS— Windows Server, Internet Information Services, SQL Server, and Windows Management Instrumentation.

Chapter 3 – Primary Site Server Installation discusses configuration options for installing SMS at a primary site, focusing on security aspects of setting up SMS.

Chapter 4 – Collections recommends security configuration protections through class and instance permissions to maintain access restrictions on collections.

Chapter 5 –Objects, Permissions, and Accounts discusses secure practices for dealing with objects and permissions and the relationship of accounts to objects and permissions.

Chapter 6 – SMS Administrator Console considers security with customized consoles and physical security protection of machines running SMS consoles. It also discusses installation of a console on a workstation from a security perspective.

Chapter 7 – SMS Client Discovery discusses security concerning methods of discovery of clients.

Chapter 8 – SMS Client Installation covers techniques of Client installation and relevant security recommendations.

Chapter 9 – Software Distribution examines security issues associated with software distribution and makes recommendations for its secure operation.

UNCLASSIFIED

Chapter 10 – Software Metering discusses the basic principles of Software Metering in SMS 2003 and recommends security configuration protections associated with it.

Chapter 11 – Remote Tools discusses the basic principles of SMS Remote Tools and their security options and recommends security protections.

Chapter 12 – Inventory Collection recommends security procedures for monitoring the inventory collection process and configuration protections for the data gathered by the inventory collection process.

Chapter 13 – Queries and Reports focuses on the principle of least privilege in setting up accounts and permissions to use query and report features.

Chapter 14 – Status and Logs gives a brief summary of these tools and security recommendations regarding their use.

Chapter 15 – Summary recapitulates the security features of SMS and the recommendations made in this paper regarding its secure configuration and use.

Appendix A – References contains a list of resources cited.

Appendix B – Glossary contains expansions of acronyms and definitions of technical terms.

Enterprise Management and Systems Management Server 2003

This chapter

- Discusses the basic principles of Enterprise Management and the role that Systems Management Server 2003 (SMS) plays within the Enterprise Management area

- Outlines the functional areas that make up Enterprise Management and applies them to Enterprise Management Systems and SMS

- Presents a number of security recommendations for Enterprise Management Systems

Enterprise Management

Enterprise Management is the administration of the various information technology (IT) components that constitute an enterprise. Enterprise Management encompasses people, business processes, transactions, policies, and automated capabilities. Enterprise Management can be partitioned into six areas.

- **Configuration Management** — Deals with setup of systems that the enterprise manages, including specific operating system and other software settings. The goal is to ensure proper setup and settings that are appropriate for and consistent with the intended operational goals of the enterprise.

- **Performance Monitoring** — Monitors the state of the network and attempts to make adjustments to improve operational efficiency.

- **Accounting** — Records information needed to bill for resource usage or to make adjustments in resource allocation.

- **Security Management** — Attempts to achieve a secure operation; it may do this in various ways, including: static means - good initial configurations of systems and user policies on use of resources; and dynamic means - periodically reviewing audit logs and configuration settings in Enterprise Management automation servers.

- **Fault Management** — Manages failures of hardware or software; the goal is to achieve 100% availability with resources in a correct state.

- **Compliance Enforcement** — Dynamically audits hardware and software configurations and settings as well as users' resource usage to ensure that enterprise policies have been properly implemented and that users are in compliance.

An Enterprise Management System is a collection of devices and computer programs that enable simplified, automated administration for the wide variety of IT components comprising an enterprise. It encompasses the automated capabilities of Enterprise Management. The network architecture of an Enterprise Management System can vary from a single central management server to a highly distributed management system, where any management server can communicate with any managed device.

An Enterprise Management System provides systematic and structured administration for infrastructure management. This is accomplished by providing management functions in the areas of Configuration, Performance, Accounting, Security, and Fault Management, as shown below in Figure 1.

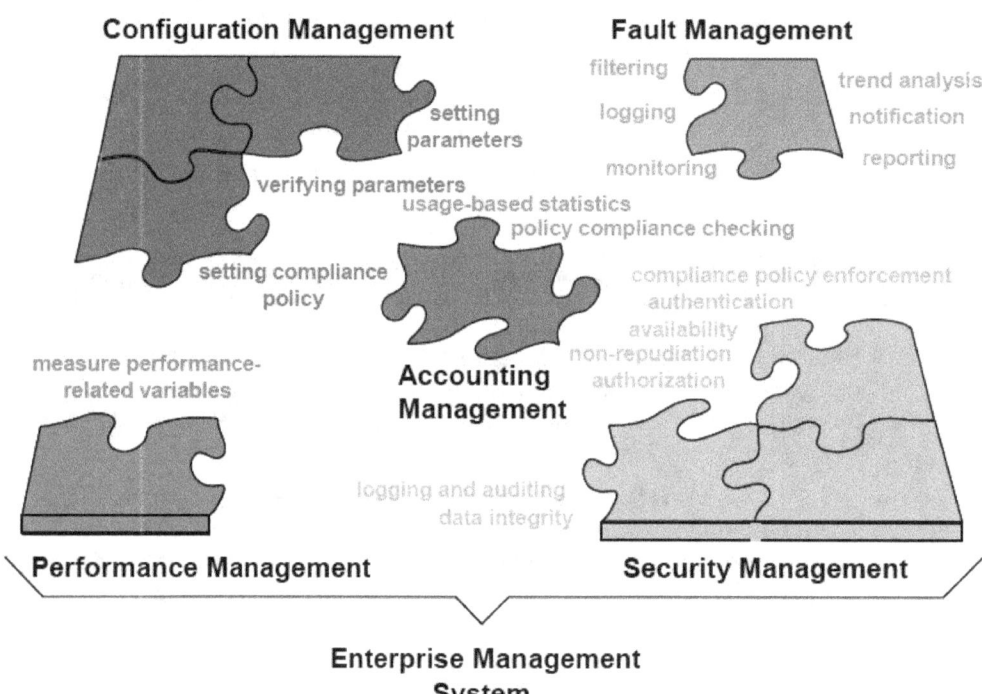

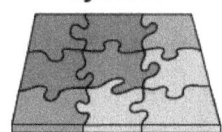

Figure 1. Enterprise Management System Functions

- Configuration Management verifies, modifies, and records information about distributed enterprise devices. This includes modifying, setting, verifying, and recording the parameters for hardware and software components of an enterprise device.

- Performance Management provides utilities that measure performance variables for enterprise devices. This performance data can be monitored to detect network problem areas and used for planning purposes.

- Accounting Management is the bookkeeper for information about the use of enterprise devices, including hardware and software components. The usage statistics can be used for software licensing administration.

- Security Management defines and implements user and access rights, monitors proper operation, and starts and stops security services. Security Management may involve authentication, authorization, data integrity, auditing, logging, non-repudiation, and availability. Note, however, that these security services apply to the Enterprise Management System's assets and processes. They are not intended to constitute a complete Enterprise Security Management system[1].

- Fault Management detects, isolates, and records malfunctions of enterprise devices and applications.

- Compliance Management defines, implements, and audits enterprise policies for users and enterprise devices and applications. Enterprise Management Systems handle the Compliance Management area with functions in Configuration, Accounting, and Security Management (as shown in Figure 1).

These functions can be provided for a range of operating systems, can be focused on a particular target operating system, and may or may not be integrated into a single package.

Not every Enterprise Management System performs all of these functions. Subsets of the functional areas just outlined can constitute useful, effective Enterprise Management Systems. Some product lines are structured specifically to allow selected products, each of which covers a specific functional area, to be integrated into an Enterprise Management System. The IBM® Tivoli® line of Enterprise Management products is an example of this.

SMS and Enterprise Management

SMS focuses on managing Windows client machines. Although SMS does not cover all the functional areas discussed previously, it does provide Windows-focused, centralized, automated administration for one or more Windows domains. Its functionality lies principally in the areas of inventory, accounting, and software distribution. Using an organization's existing network, it automates hardware and software inventory, product compliance, software distribution and installation, and software metering. It also provides remote tools and diagnostic tools to assist in managing the organization's resources. Figure 2 broadly depicts how the functions of SMS relate to general Enterprise Management functionality. The functions in the blue call-outs are SMS functions.

---

[1] Enterprise Security Management deals with a wide range of functions and several layers in an enterprise's operations. It manages the security of the entire enterprise, including: devices, such as firewalls, intrusion detectors, and routers; the networking infrastructure; applications; transactions; business processes; and policy.

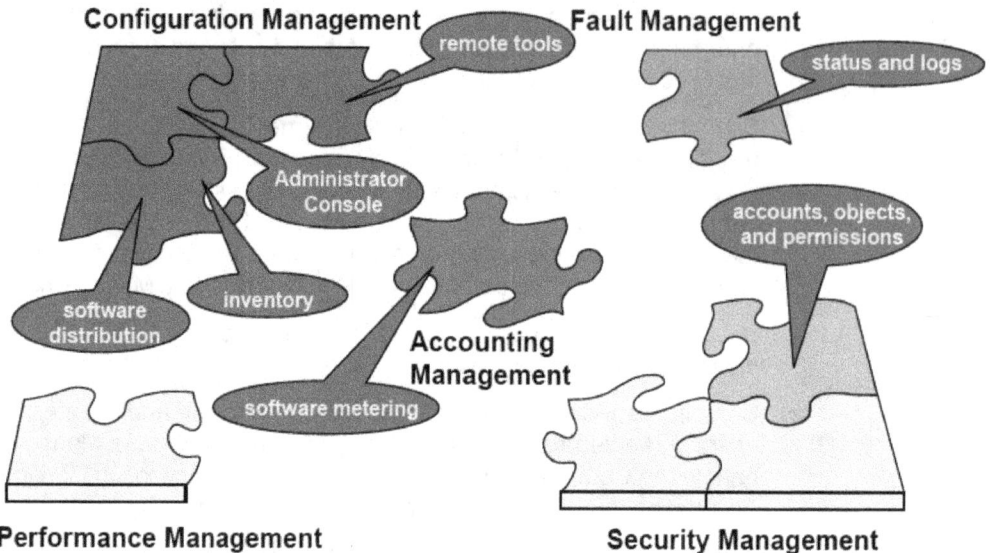

Configuration Management   **Fault Management**

remote tools

status and logs

Administrator
Console

accounts, objects,
and permissions

software
distribution

inventory

**Accounting
Management**

software metering

Performance Management   **Security Management**

Figure 2. SMS Functions in the Context of Enterprise Management

SMS covers a subset of the functional areas of Enterprise Management. The subset of functionality is driven by the particular focus of SMS—managing certain aspects of the operation of Windows clients in one or more Windows domains. A functional area that is not covered by SMS, Performance Management, is covered by another Microsoft product called Microsoft Operations Manager (MOM). This product provides event management, proactive monitoring and alerting, reporting, and trend analysis for Windows systems.

SMS provides Enterprise Management functionality through a service called the SMS Administrator Console. This console is used to view all aspects of an SMS installation, to configure and use SMS features, configure SMS sites, maintain the site database, and monitor the status of an SMS hierarchy. The console combines all the SMS management functions to provide an integrated Enterprise Management System for Windows clients. Although not a comprehensive Enterprise Management solution, Systems Management Server provides a single management focal point for a number of Enterprise Management functions and can be cost effective for many organizations.

An Enterprise Management System is a powerful tool. With this power comes the obligation to examine and deal with the security issues that naturally arise.

Security Guidance

The security recommendations in this guide focus on configuring and using SMS 2003. Although specific to SMS 2003, many of the security recommendations can be generalized, making them applicable to other Enterprise Management Systems. Enterprise Management Systems generally have many management functions in common. Cutting across these management functions are security focus areas in which security recommendations can be made.

The security focus areas are:

UNCLASSIFIED

- **Authentication** provides the means to verify the identity of a client through the exchange of information.
- **Access Control** provides the means to grant access to system resources based on the identity of the user.
- **Availability** provides the means to ensure that system data is available to users when required.
- **Integrity** provides the means to protect system data from accidental or purposeful alteration in transit.
- **Confidentiality** provides the means to ensure that data is protected from accidental or purposeful disclosure.
- **Auditing and Logging** provide the means to ensure that actions performed by all users, authorized or otherwise, are recorded.
- **Security Control** provides the means to ensure that enterprise security policies have been set consistently within a domain.

Using these security focus areas, general security configuration guidance for Enterprise Management Systems can be determined. The security recommendations shown in Table 1 are generalizations of important security points that apply to SMS 2003 and appear later in this guide. Thus, an Enterprise Management administrator using a product other than SMS can find valuable ideas about secure configuration and operation in this guide.

Table 1. General Security Recommendations

Security Area	Recommendations
Authentication Accountability	Set up specific accounts in accord with the principle of least privilege[2]. Use strong passwords for management accounts.
Access Control	Enforce separation of administrative duties by giving administrators access only to those functions and objects that are necessary to perform their roles. Set permissions on system folders and files that contain system information to be as restrictive as possible, consistent with usage by the role that manages them.
Availability	Ensure that Enterprise Management system information is available for operational use; for example, use log files to audit availability of services. To avoid denial of service, use the available administrative tools of the system to ensure that settings for all services are correct. Also, periodically review all settings as changes are made to any of the settings to ensure continued interoperability of the services.
Integrity	Protect Enterprise Management system information from accidental and malicious loss and corruption; for example, use access control and/or cryptographic means to preserve the integrity of vital operational data. Use available cryptographic methods, as necessary, to protect critical information that is transmitted over the network.
Confidentiality	Configuration of certain options on client systems can affect the extent to which client system users are aware of and/or participate in various Enterprise Management actions initiated from the Enterprise Management system control console. Carefully select such options to accurately reflect enterprise policy for client systems and their users.
Audit/Logging	Enable logging of the operations of system servers and/or services, collecting only enough data to meet the needs of the risk environment in which the system operates. Verify the operation of system servers and/or services by periodically reviewing their status in their respective logs.
Security Control	In situations where multiple systems are involved across domains and/or in a multi-tiered hierarchy, review settings that may be propagated or inherited to ensure that resulting configurations are consistent with enterprise security policy.

---

[2]   The principle of least privilege calls for giving the minimum permissions needed by users to perform their authorized roles.

UNCLASSIFIED

Architectural Considerations

This chapter provides security recommendations relating to the general deployment of SMS 2003 in a site hierarchy, succinctly referred to as its architecture.

Architectural Terminology

Some essential terms need to be understood in discussing SMS. They are introduced here in an order that provides an overview of the overall architecture of SMS and the site that it serves. The glossary in this document has the definitions in alphabetical order and should prove helpful to readers not already intimately familiar with SMS.

An **SMS site** defines the computers, users, groups, and other resources that are managed by SMS. The **SMS Site Server** is the Windows server (2000 or 2003) on which SMS has been installed. An **SMS site system** is a Windows server that performs one or more of the following SMS roles for an SMS site:

- Management Point
- Client Access Point
- Server Locator Point (replaces SMS 2.0 Logon Point)
- Distribution Point
- Reporting Point
- Software Metering server

An **SMS Management Point** (MP) is an SMS site system that services SMS Advanced Clients on behalf of an SMS Site Server. An **SMS Client Access Point** (CAP) provides the same functionality for SMS Legacy Clients. An **SMS Server Locator Point** is an SMS site system that locates CAPs and MPs for SMS clients. An **SMS Distribution Point** is any server that stores the package files, programs, and scripts necessary for a package to execute successfully at an SMS client computer. An **SMS Reporting Point** is an SMS site system that hosts the code for the SMS Report Viewer and any supplemental reports. An **SMS Software Metering Server** is an SMS site system that supports monitoring of software running on computers within the SMS site to detect and report use of computer programs within the SMS site.

SMS 2003 relies on Internet Information Services (IIS) to support the Management Point, Server Locator Point, and Reporting Point site systems. The Distribution Point also uses IIS when BITS (discussed in the Software Distribution chapter) is enabled. **IIS** is a web server used to publish and distribute web-based content to standard browsers and other systems. It provides publishing services such as WWW, FTP, and SMTP.

An **SMS client** is any computer that is supported by SMS, has been assigned to an SMS site, and has SMS client software installed. Client software is contained in the SMS Advanced Client and the SMS Legacy Client. The **SMS Advanced Client** is the new client-agent package in SMS 2003. It includes all the client agents to support SMS

UNCLASSIFIED

functions provided in the SMS Legacy Client, as well as new features and enhanced security. The **SMS Legacy Client** is a legacy client-agent package containing the client agents needed to carry out SMS functions at an SMS client, such as software distribution and inventory collection; it is based on the SMS 2.0 Client.

An **SMS administrator** is the individual trusted with the implementation, maintenance, and support of an SMS site or specific objects in the SMS database. The SMS Administrator Console is a Microsoft Management Console (MMC) with the SMS Administrator snap-in added.

An **SMS site hierarchy** resembles an organizational flowchart and exists whenever two or more SMS sites have been defined in a parent-child relationship. An **SMS primary site** is an SMS site that stores its own SMS data and all the sites beneath in a SQL Server® database, which is called the **SMS Site Database**. **SQL Server** is a relational database server that can be installed on a Microsoft Windows (NT or later) system.

Primary sites have administrative tools, such as the SMS Administrator Console, that enable the SMS Administrator to directly manage the site. An **SMS secondary site** is an SMS site that does not have an SMS Site Database. An SMS secondary site is always a child of a primary site and is administered solely through its parent or through another primary site above it in the SMS site hierarchy. An **SMS central site** is an SMS primary site that resides at the top of the SMS site hierarchy—not a child to any other site.

Architectural Security

To ensure that as few processes as possible have the enhanced privileges of the system's computer account, which allow access to SMS files and data, do not install other services that use the LocalSystem account on Site Servers and systems. Additional discussion is in the Security section of Microsoft's security document for SMS. [11]

In providing its systems management functionality, SMS uses other systems or technologies. As a result, its secure operation depends to some extent on the secure operation of these supporting technologies. Windows Server, Internet Information Services, SQL Server, and Windows Management Instrumentation, in addition to physical and network security, support the SMS security environment. In addition, some general aspects of SMS deployment and use must be considered when establishing secure operations.

Windows Server

SMS depends on the underlying operating system. Not only does it depend on it for managing the server hardware and its connections to the site network, it also uses the operating system's file sharing to communicate among SMS sites, SMS component servers, and with SMS clients. As discussed in Microsoft documentation [see Reference 1], specific aspects of the operating system that affect SMS security are

- Account security
- Accounts and processes
- Permissions and access control
- Account authentication

Numerous sources of guidance for configuring and operating Windows operating systems, usually with at least some consideration of security, are available. Use them as needed to ensure that the Windows server on which SMS runs is hardened and operating

UNCLASSIFIED

securely. Apply the security guidance, as suitable, provided by Microsoft for Windows Server 2003. This document has been reviewed and endorsed by the NSA. [9]

Internet Information Services (IIS)

IIS security is especially important when the site is running in SMS advanced security mode. In this mode, the Site Server's computer account must be granted administrative privileges on each site system in the site. IIS services are required to run under the local system account in an SMS environment. The SMS Site Server uses the local system account to manage its local files and registry settings. Thus, processes running in the local system account context of IIS can access those files and registry settings. Therefore, to ensure that potential weaknesses in IIS do not compromise the SMS Site Server, install site systems that require IIS separate from the Site Server. Also, required IIS components differ among site system roles. Therefore, to minimize potential avenues of attack against a single system, install each site system requiring IIS on a separate machine with only the IIS components required by the site system role. If this is not possible, install site system roles requiring IIS on one server. The required IIS components for each SMS role using IIS is as follows:

- Management Points – BITS Server Extensions

- Server Locator Point – Default IIS install

- Reporting Point – Active Server Pages (reports with graphs also require Microsoft Office 2000 SP2 or Office XP)

- Distribution Points with BITS enabled – IIS and WebDAV

IIS 6.0 running on a Windows 2003 platform is preferred over earlier versions of IIS. IIS 6.0 and Windows 2003 are significantly more secure out-of-the-box. Sites that cannot accommodate this recommendation can harden the IIS servers by following the guidance provided by Microsoft for securing IIS (see IIS security checklist in Microsoft's *Scenarios and Procedures for Microsoft Systems Management Server 2003: Security* [11]) and the IIS security guidance provided by the NSA. [7] A template is available to assist in securing IIS in an SMS environment that adheres to the guidance provided by these documents. IIS Lockdown 2.1 Template (which includes a URLScan template) is used in SMS environments with IIS 5 and the URLScan 2.5 Template is used in SMS environments with IIS 6. Running these tools without using the SMS templates can cause SMS operations to fail.

IIS anonymous access is not required for most SMS site system roles that use IIS. Configure these components to use Integrated Windows authentication. For Distribution Points, ensure users designated to access packages have read permissions and the account used by the SMS Distribution Manager service (computer account for advanced security) has full control on the package directory. The Management Point is the only site system role that MUST be configured to allow anonymous access. The anonymous account also requires access to the ccm_incoming, ccm_outgoing, ccm_system and sms_mp virtual directories of the Management Point. Permissions granted on these directories to the anonymous account (IUSR_machinename) when a system is designated as a Management Point are adequate and do not need to change. If a change is required on the IIS directories for any site system role, including moving them to another NTFS drive or partition, remove the SMS site system role, make the changes and add the role back to the system.

> Warning: Do not configure IIS to use SSL on SMS site systems. SMS components are not capable of being configured to use HTTPS.

UNCLASSIFIED

SQL Server

SMS uses SQL Server to manage an SMS site database. The integrity of this critical resource must be protected. Even though multiple sites are capable of sharing a single SQL Server, it is recommended each site maintain its own SQL Server database. Since components of SMS require direct access to the database over a network, exposure to integrity and denial of service attacks is increased. To minimize this exposure, segregate the SMS database server from all other SQL Server databases and applications not related to SMS. In addition, install SQL Server on the SMS primary Site Server to cut down on network traffic, thereby reducing the risk of SQL to SMS traffic being captured or replayed.

There are two options governing how SMS will access the SQL Server database: Standard and Integrated. These options, which are available during SMS installation, determine how SMS components will authenticate to the SQL Server database – using SQL Server authentication (Standard) or Windows integrated authentication (Integrated). SQL Server authentication is weak. Therefore, it is recommended Integrated be selected and SQL Server authentication be disabled in an advanced security SMS environment. To ensure this weak authentication method cannot be used, at a minimum install the site server database with SQL Server 2000, service pack 3, running in **Windows only** authentication mode as opposed to **SQL Server and Windows** authentication mode (which permits SQL login IDs and passwords). Although SQL Server's "sa" account is not used in **Windows only** authentication mode, a password for this account must be assigned during installation of the server. Ensure that a strong password is assigned for this account. (See reference [4] for more information pertaining to the secure configuration and administration of SQL Server 2000.)

To follow the guidance of least privilege for accounts, use a low privileged domain user account as the SQL Server service account. To use a domain user account, fully qualified domain name (FQDN) and NetBIOS Service Principal Name (SPN), entries must be created for the account. Either the setspn command or ADSI Edit tool can be used to create these entries. See Microsoft Knowledge Base Article 829868 for how-to instructions.

Windows Management Instrumentation (WMI) and the SMS Provider

Windows Management Instrumentation (WMI) is the Microsoft implementation of Web-based Enterprise Management (WBEM), a collection of technologies designed to facilitate management of an enterprise. The WMI management infrastructure in Windows supports monitoring and controlling system resources through a common set of interfaces and provides an organized, consistent model of Windows operation, configuration, and status.

SMS uses the WMI management interface on clients for hardware inventory collection, on servers as an interface to the SMS site database, and on consoles as an interface to the SMS site database. SMS also uses WMI for storing some configuration data, such as that used by Network Trace. WMI supports full security for the Windows NT 4.0, Windows 2000, Windows XP, and Windows Server 2003 families, and limited security for Windows 98. Discussion of WMI namespaces and security descriptors is beyond the scope of this document. For an overview of SMS object security and WMI, see Microsoft's *Scenarios and Procedures for Microsoft Systems Management Server 2003: Security* [11], Appendix A.

The SMS Provider, through WMI, processes requests for data from the SMS site database, either from the SMS Administrator Console or programmatically—via a program written in the .NET framework for example. The SMS Provider can be installed

UNCLASSIFIED

on the same computer as the SMS Site Server or the SMS site database. Microsoft recommends that you install both the SMS Provider and the SMS site database on the Site Server.

While SMS generally relies on other technologies to enforce security—the operating system for example—SMS itself enforces security through the SMS Provider. For example, the SMS Provider checks the SMS security permissions of a user who is attempting to access an SMS object. The SMS Provider enforces SMS object security whether access to SMS objects is through the SMS Administrator Console or through a program that accesses SMS through WMI.

The SMS Administrators Group has access to the SMS Provider. Access is needed for viewing and modifying SMS security objects and data in the SMS Administrator Console or similar tools. By default, members of the SMS Administrators Group on the local computer and members of the local Administrators group have access.

> WARNING: Be careful about adding to this group, which is a windows group, not one within SMS. This group has the ability to interact (only as public) with the database and interact with the SMS provider (including remotely interacting with the provider). Thus, users in this group will have access to the database and WMI provider and should be carefully selected. No unnecessary users should be present in the group.

Detailed discussion of the SMS Provider and WMI is beyond the scope of this document. For additional information, see Microsoft documentation—for example, the Concepts, Planning, and Deployment Guide and the SMS 2003 SDK Documentation. [1, 7]

The important architectural consideration in this context is to install the SMS Provider on the primary Site Server, the same server where it is recommended SQL Server be installed. Choice of installation location is provided during SMS installation.

Network Security

Because of the network traffic that necessarily flows among sites, create the least number of sites required for your environment, as discussed in Microsoft's *Scenarios and Procedures for Microsoft Systems Management Server 2003: Security*. [11]

To protect against attackers sending bogus site control data, and for other network security reasons, enable secure key exchange. Refer to Microsoft's *Scenarios and Procedures for Microsoft Systems Management Server 2003: Security*. [11]

> NOTE: If you have SMS 2.0 servers in your site hierarchy, check the Disable communications with SMS 2.0 SP4 or lower sites checkbox; install SP5 to get signed communications with SMS 2003 servers; this will also allow you to use secure key exchange with SMS 2.0 sites.

In addition, use Internet Protocol Security (IPSEC) to encrypt communications between site systems and the Site Server. See the referenced Microsoft security document for SMS and the NSA Guide on IPSEC. [11, 10]

❑ Do not install other services that use the LocalSystem account on Site Servers and systems.

❑ Apply the security guidance of the applicable NSA guides to the operating system (Windows Server 2000 or Windows Server 2003) used by the site's installation of SMS 2003 and the security guidance provided by Microsoft for Windows Server 2003 as appropriate. [9, 10]

❑ Apply the security guidance of the NSA guide for IIS. [7] Also, check the guidance provided by Microsoft for securing IIS and the IIS Security Checklist in *Scenarios and Procedures for Microsoft Systems Management Server 2003: Security.* [11]

❑ Install SQL Server on the SMS primary Site Server and do not use it for any other application.

❑ Use a non-privileged domain user account to run the SQL Server services. Use the setspn command or ADSI Edit tool to configure the FQDN and SPN entries for this account in active Directory.

❑ Assign a strong password for the SQL Server sa account even though integrated Windows authentication mode is used.

❑ Use the SMS Integrated security option for SQL Server access.

❑ Apply the security recommendations of the NSA guide on SQL Server. [4]

❑ Install the SMS Provider on the primary Site Server where SQL Server is also installed.

❑ Carefully select any users to be added to the SMS Administrators Group and make sure that no unnecessary users are in the group.

❑ Create the fewest sites required for your environment.

❑ Enable secure key exchange.

❑ Use Internet Protocol Security (IPSEC) to encrypt communications between site systems and the Site Server. (Do not configure SSL for IIS on SMS site system components per warning in the IIS section).

❑ Use Windows Server 2003 and IIS 6.0. If you use Windows Server 2000, lock it down using the NSA security guidance. [10]

❑ Keep IIS-systems separate from non-IIS systems.

❑ If possible, have a separate server for each SMS role that requires IIS. If not, combine roles requiring IIS on one or more servers and do not assign other roles to the server(s).

UNCLASSIFIED

Primary Site Server Installation

This chapter discusses configuration options for installing SMS at a primary site. It focuses on those installation issues that are particularly relevant from a security perspective and highlights some aspects of installation to establish context for the rest of this guide.

Installation of SMS begins with its installation at a primary site. SMS Setup creates each primary site as a stand-alone site, which can have multiple secondary sites, all of which propagate data to the primary site. During SMS installation, Express or Custom installation must be selected.

Express installation installs and activates all functions, whereas Custom installs only the basic Site Server and SMS Administrator Console. However, all other functions and options can be selected during Custom installation. Any such functions selected under Custom installation are installed but not enabled. Also, aside from optional selections of functions, more things are installed disabled by default under Custom installation than under Express installation, such as Discovery Techniques. Use custom installation to ensure that unnecessary functions are not installed and activated. During custom installation, install only necessary SMS functions. For example, if your site does not require the use of Remote Tools[3], do not install them. Once installed, a function cannot be uninstalled without removing and reinstalling SMS. Thus, Custom installation is a better choice from a security point of view.

Also, do not install SMS on a domain controller because a break-in to SMS operating in this situation can give access to sensitive domain information residing on the domain controller. This, in turn, can facilitate attacks on other computers in the domain.

Security Mode

During installation, an option to choose advanced or standard security mode is available. Advanced security mode relies on the use of the local System account to run services and it uses the computer accounts to communicate among servers. This eliminates the need for SMS to use password-managed accounts. SMS 2003 standard security mode is similar to SMS 2.0 security. In standard security mode, SMS relies on password-managed user accounts[4] to run services, to make changes to computers, and to connect between computers.

Select advanced security mode as it provides better security. The reasons for this will become clear in Chapter 5, which deals with objects, permissions, and accounts.

> NOTE: If standard security is required at your site, apply the
> recommendations of the SMS 2.0 Security Guide. [6]

---

[3]   See the chapter Remote Tools and Microsoft's SMS Documentation to determine whether Remote Tools will be necessary.
[4]   As opposed to the use of the local system account and the computer accounts in advanced security.

Advanced security mode uses Active Directory. For an SMS 2003 site to use advanced security mode, the Site Server must be running Windows Server 2000 or Windows Server 2003 in an Active Directory domain. Installation of SMS 2003 in advanced security mode is not possible in a Windows NT 4.0 domain. Also, to use advanced security, the site must be a primary site or it must be reporting to a site in advanced security mode. Finally, the SMS 2003 site SQL servers must be running SQL Server 2000 SP3 or later.

The following configurations are supported for advanced security mode:

- SMS 2003 advanced security site reporting to an SMS 2003 advanced security site

- SMS 2003 standard security site reporting to an SMS 2003 advanced security site

- SMS 2.0 site reporting to an SMS 2003 advanced security site

Secondary Site Server Installation

A secondary Site Server can be installed from the SMS 2003 compact disc, or by connecting to an image of that compact disc on a mapped network drive, hard disk, or a removable drive of the secondary site. A secondary site can also be installed from the primary Site Server using the SMS Administrator Console and the Site Installation Wizard. Unless the installation is done locally, the computer account of the primary Site Server must be added to the local Administrators group of the secondary Site Server and vice versa. Install secondary Site Servers locally to avoid giving the primary Site Server's computer account administrator privileges on the secondary Site Server.

Operate secondary Site Servers in advanced security mode.

Registry Keys

On the Site Server, installation creates an **SMS** key under the **HKEY_LOCAL_MACHINE\SOFTWARE\Microsoft** key in the Registry and the **SMS** key has many subkeys. The **Power Users** group has permissions on the **SMS** key and various permissions, including **Delete**, on its subkeys through special permissions. In general, these permissions are excessive. If there is no need to assign any users to the **Power Users** group, remove the **Power Users** group from the **SMS** key and all its subkeys. If the Power Users group must be retained for some operational reason, reduce its permissions throughout this **SMS** branch of the Registry to **Read** permission only.

> WARNING: If for some reason you retain the permissions of the Power Users group throughout this branch, be aware that Power Users have Full control on the
> HKEY_LOCAL_MACHINE\SOFTWARE\Microsoft\SMS\Client\Client Components\Remote Control key via the special permissions.

In addition, the **Everyone** group has **Full control** on the **HKEY_LOCAL_MACHINE\SOFTWARE\Microsoft\SMS\Client\Client Components\Remote Control\User Settings** key, again excessive permission. Replace the **Everyone** group with the **Authenticated Users** group, retaining **Full control**.

Important Security Points

- ❏ Use custom installation.

- ❏ Ensure that unnecessary SMS functions are not installed.

- ❏ Do not install SMS on a domain controller.

- ❏ Select advanced security mode during installation of SMS.

- ❏ Apply the recommendations of the SMS 2.0 Security Guide if standard security mode is required at your site.

- ❏ Install secondary Site Servers locally.

- ❏ Operate secondary Site Servers in advanced security mode.

- ❏ Under the Registry key **HKEY_LOCAL_MACHINE\SOFTWARE\Microsoft\,** remove the **Power Users** group from the **SMS** key and all its subkeys. If the Power Users group must be retained for some operational reason, reduce its permissions on this **SMS** and its subkeys to **Read** permission only.

- ❏ Replace the **Everyone** group with the **Authenticated Users** group on the Registry key **HKEY_LOCAL_MACHINE\SOFTWARE\Microsoft\SMS\Client\Client Components\Remote Control\User Settings**, retaining **Full control**.

Collections

This chapter focuses on security for Collections, whose integrity and confidentiality must be protected to reduce the risk of unauthorized modification and the risk of an intruder leveraging the information for attack purposes.

Overview

Secure use of Collections depends on a basic understanding of their purpose. SMS uses Collections to organize SMS resources. A Collection is a customized view of SMS site resources. Collections group resources based on membership rules, providing groupings of like machines, users, user groups, or other SMS resources. They are used to organize software distribution, display inventory data, and create organizational boundaries.

Collections can be customized using specific criteria to represent tasks that must be performed on particular targets. They can also be used to limit security rights to specific SMS resources.

Collection membership can be either direct or query-based. A direct-membership collection must be manually maintained. A query-based membership is dynamic in nature. The resources for direct membership are defined using the Create Direct Membership Rule Wizard. For query-based membership, membership rules are defined by an SMS query and SMS keeps the collection up-to-date by periodically running the query. Query-based memberships are more practical and efficient.

Security

Default collections are created during SMS Site Server installation. These collections are used to group resources into easily managed components, organized by operating systems and users. Delete any default collections that will not be used, in accord with the best practice of eliminating unnecessary functions, objects, and so on. The specific danger here is that an attacker could use these maliciously since an attacker seeing a default collection knows exactly what query was used to create that collection. Since unneeded default collections are not used, they may not be monitored as closely as the risk posture would warrant. Default collections may also be more useful to an attacker looking to have widespread impact versus the specific, custom collections that are more likely to be used by legitimate administrators. In any case, custom collections can always be created to meet your needs, so there is no harm in deleting a default collection whose functionality is needed later.

As suggested in the figure, the Collections object is a class, a particular Collection is an instance of the Collections Class, and a member of a Collection is a resource.

UNCLASSIFIED

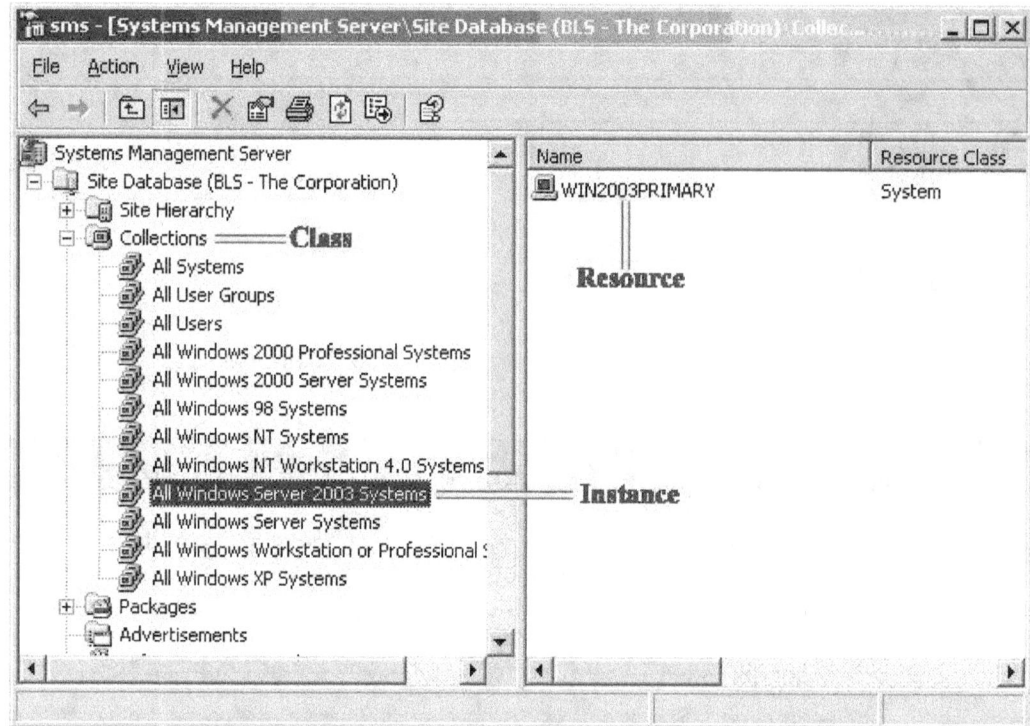

Figure 3. Class, Instance, and Resource Relationships

Collections can be created using the SMS Administrator Console. A new collection inherits the security settings of the Collections class. The Security tab of the new collection properties allows instance security to be set for the new collection. All objects in the collection receive the security settings of the instance. See *Chapter 5: Objects, Permissions, and Accounts* for a discussion of how different class and instance permissions are reconciled.

Unlike other SMS objects, with the Collections class object you can grant permissions for the resources in a collection—Delete Resource, Modify Resource, Read Resource, Use Remote Tools, and View Collected Files. These permissions are available for setting at both the class and instance levels. When you grant resource permissions in a particular collection, it is for all resources in that collection, not for individual resources. For example, if a user has Delete Resource permission for collection A, the user can delete any of the resources in collection A.

By default, the Administrator and System accounts are given all permissions for the Collections class. Thus, these accounts have full control over all resources in all instances of the Collections class. The creator of an instance by default is given full permission (read, modify, and delete) over the instance. When roles are assigned for controlling instances of the Collections class, remove the unneeded default permissions that have been assigned by SMS.

Note that if you grant permissions to a user for resources in a collection, the permissions extend to the same resources contained in other collections. This is regardless of the permissions that the user has for the other collections. For example, if you grant a user Modify Resource permission for the All Windows 98 Systems collection, that user can modify clients running Windows 98 contained in any collection.

> WARNING: Use care when granting permissions to resources to ensure that undesired side effects do not occur.

UNCLASSIFIED

Use class and instance security to maintain access restrictions on collections, in accord with the principle of least privilege. Implementing class and instance security can restrict user access to collections. Since class, instance, and resource security settings are cumulative, and resource permissions can span instances, resulting in the most permissive resource privileges, take special care to ensure proper control over collections.

Before performing an operation on a collection, such as distributing an advertisement, verify the membership of the collection.

Important Security Points

- ❑ Delete any default collections that will not be used.
- ❑ When roles are assigned for controlling instances of the Collections class, remove the unneeded default permissions that have been assigned by SMS.
- ❑ Use class and instance security permissions to maintain access restrictions on collections, applying the principle of least privilege in assigning the permissions.
- ❑ Take special care to ensure proper control over collections with respect to the possible interactions affecting resource privileges.
- ❑ Verify the membership in collections before using the collections with SMS functions, such as software distribution.

Objects, Permissions, and Accounts

> WARNING: In some cases, SMS assigns rights for the
> LocalSystem account - NT Authority\SYSTEM that are
> not used in this version of SMS. Do not remove those
> rights as future versions or tools might require those
> rights.

This chapter discusses objects and permissions and their relationship to SMS accounts, focusing on secure practice in setting and reviewing permissions.

As suggested in Chapter 3, use advanced security mode if feasible for your operation. The way accounts are managed by SMS 2003 in advanced security mode provides better security than the way they are managed in standard security mode. One of the advantages of advanced security mode is that it does not require accounts other than the local System and the computer account. For example, it uses the local System account to run services and the computer account for communications. Local System and computer accounts are automatically maintained by the operating system, which ensures that no user can know their passwords and no manual maintenance is required. Although there may be site hierarchies where only standard security mode is available, this chapter discusses security assuming that advanced security mode is in effect.

Objects and Permissions

There are eight types of SMS objects

- Advertisements
- Collections
- Packages
- Reports
- Queries
- Sites
- Software Metering Rules
- Status Messages

Permissions can be set at two levels in the SMS object hierarchy: class and instance. The class level grants users permissions for all instances in a specific class—for example, all packages or all collections. The instance level grants permissions for a specific instance of an object type (class) such as the "All Systems" collection. In both cases, permissions are assigned per user or per user group.

For example, the class-level Read right on the Collections class enables the user having the right to see all the collections and the members of each collection. The instance-level

UNCLASSIFIED

Read right on a particular collection enables the user having the right to see that collection and its members.

Class and instance permissions are cumulative across instances and they combine to produce the maximum level of permissions from the class and instance permissions for a given instance. For example, if a user has Read permission on "All System" and Use Remote Tools permission on "All Windows 98 Systems", then the user has both Read and Use Remote Tools permission on all systems that are members of both collections.

Since SMS rights are cumulative, if a user has class security rights to an SMS object type and conflicting instance security rights to an instance of that type, SMS reconciles the class and instance rights to grant the highest level of permissions. For example, if a user has full permissions at the package class level and Read permission to an instance of the package class, the user's effective permissions are full permissions to all packages, including the instance for which the user has Read permission only set at the instance level.

Permissions granted to both class and instance rights could create confusion. Limit areas where both class and instance permissions are assigned. When both are assigned, verify that the least restrictive settings, based on class and instance reconciliation, are acceptable for each security right. Also, refer to the Microsoft document, which provides additional suggestions on setting the permissions. [11, **The SMS Object Security Rights section**]

Table 2. Available Permissions and Their Object Types

Permission	Object Type	Capability
Administer	All object types	Administer all object classes, including assigning or modifying security permissions.
Advertise	Collection	Advertise to entities in a collection. This permission does not grant the ability to create advertisements. That ability requires Create permission on the advertisement object type.
Create	All object types	Create an instance of an object type, such as a new query or collection.
Delegate	All object types	Delegate permission on an object for a particular user allows that user to grant permissions on the object to other users. The only permissions that the user can grant are the permissions that the user has on that object.
Delete	All object types except Status Messages	Delete an instance of an object type, such as a package or an advertisement.
Delete Resource	Collection	Delete a resource from a collection, such as a computer.
Distribute	Package	Deploy a package to a Distribution Point.

UNCLASSIFIED

Permission	Object Type	Capability
Manage SQL Commands	Site	Create, modify, and delete site SQL commands.
Manage Status Filters	Site	Create, modify, and delete status filter rules.
Meter	Site	Apply Software Metering rules to the site.
Modify	All object types except Status Message	Make changes to an object, such as editing the query statement for a query.
Modify Resource	Collection	Modify a resource in a collection.
Read	All object types except Status Message	View an instance and its properties.
Read Resource	Collection	View a resource in a collection.
Use Remote Tools	Collection	Initiate a Remote Tools session with a client in a collection.
View Collected Files	Collection	View the files collected from a client through the Resource Explorer.

SMS object permissions are cumulative across collections as well as across class and instance permissions on a given object. For example, if a user has the Read right on Collection A and the Use Remote Tools right on Collection B, then the user has the Read and Use Remote Tools rights on all systems that are members of both collections.

In accord with the principle of least privilege, tightly control access to SMS objects. SMS administrators should be able to manipulate only those sites, packages, advertisements, and other SMS objects that are appropriate to their roles. Periodic reviews of access permissions, by inspection of SMS class and instance security permissions, can assure that the principle of least privilege is effectively applied.

Accounts

For a given class, at least one account must have Administer permission to that class in order for administrators to set permissions for that class. If this condition is not met, administrators are effectively locked out from setting permissions on that class and any instances of it that exist. SMS provides two safeguards in this regard: it prevents one from removing the last account with Administer permission to a class and it prevents users from removing their own Administer permissions. When a new instance of an object is created, the user creating the object is automatically assigned Read, Modify, and Delete permissions for that instance and the Distribute permission if the object is a package. Granting Administer permission does not automatically grant the other permissions.

Two accounts are initially given full permissions to all object types: the Windows System account on the local machine and the account used to install SMS.

Accounts can be added and permissions to SMS classes and instances can be granted using the **Security Rights** console item in the SMS Administrator Console. From this console, rights can also be copied from an existing SMS user or SMS group to the new user being created.

Permissions can also be modified by using the **Security Tab** of the **Properties** page of the class, object, or instance or by using the **SMS User Wizard** task. Users who do not have permissions for various classes or instances do not see those objects in their SMS Administrator Console. Users who have partial permissions for SMS Administrator Console items see only those items for which they have permissions.

Important Security Points

- ❑ Limit areas where both class and instance permissions are assigned.

- ❑ Verify that the least restrictive settings, based on class and instance reconciliation, are acceptable for each security right.

- ❑ Check that SMS administrators can manipulate only sites, packages, advertisements, and other SMS objects that they are authorized to manipulate.

- ❑ Inspect the SMS class and instance security permissions with the SMS Administrator Console and further restrict access to specific roles, applying the principle of least privilege.

UNCLASSIFIED

SMS Administrator Console

This chapter discusses customized consoles and security considerations associated with them.

Administrator Console Overview

The SMS Administrator Console is a snap-in to the Microsoft Management Console (MMC). Like other snap-ins, the SMS Administrator Console can be run in Author mode to allow customization. The SMS Administrator Console looks like a Windows Explorer window. The console tree, in the left pane of the window, displays objects that can be accessed and managed by the SMS administrator. As an object is selected in the left pane, the contents of that object are displayed in the right pane. The contents may consist of additional objects that can be accessed and maintained.

The SMS Administrator Console has two menus: Action and View. Selecting an object and choosing the Action menu displays the Action menu options for that object. These options can include opening the item (same as double-clicking it), refreshing the object (updating its contents or properties), deleting the object, and performing some additional task such as displaying messages or launching a tool. Most objects have Properties windows in which their attributes can be viewed and changed. Right-clicking an object displays the object's context menu, which lists the same options as the Action menu. Author mode allows customization of the console.

Customization

On SMS primary Site Servers, the directories that contain the SMS console files are accessible by all users in the SMS Admins group[5]. Good security practice suggests creating a custom SMS console for SMS administrators with only specialized, restricted roles. A custom console can give access only to those classes and instances that are necessary for the administrator's role. Administrators running custom consoles on remote machines do not require administrator rights on the primary Site Server. However, they do require membership in the SMS Admins group.

> WARNING: If the user of a custom console on the primary Site Server is a member of the Windows Server 2003 local administrators group, which is often the case, the user can, if so inclined, subvert the restrictions of the role imposed on them by the custom console.

---

[5] This group is created during installation of SMS.

Custom consoles can be created using the Microsoft Management Console (MMC). Prior to creating the custom console, create user groups and user accounts based on SMS administrator roles. In MMC, create a custom console with the functionality necessary for each SMS administrator role. Save each console as a file with a .msc extension and distribute each one to the appropriate administrator. The SMS software distribution feature can be used to distribute and install the software or the local administrator can install the software required for the custom console. Be aware, to install a custom console on a remote machine, the SMS Setup must be run. This means SMS binaries will be available on the remote machine. With these binaries available to them, it is possible for local administrators to create their own SMS site.

Ideally, SMS Administrator consoles will be on machines that are physically protected from unauthorized access. However, if this is not possible, secure them when a staff member is not physically present. Using a password-protected screensaver to lock the workstation soon after user activity stops can help to ensure that the workstation is secure.

Important Security Points

❑ Consider distributing administrator functions by creating custom consoles, giving administrators access only to those functions and objects necessary to perform their assigned roles.

❑ Physically secure any machine running SMS Administrator Console.

❑ If the machine running the SMS Administrator Console cannot be physically secured, secure SMS Administrator Console sessions with a password-protected screen saver.

UNCLASSIFIED

SMS Client Discovery

This chapter discusses SMS client discovery, covering the methods of discovery and relevant security points.

> NOTE: This chapter (SMS Client Discovery) and the installation chapter (SMS Client Installation) both deal with "clients", but the "clients" being addressed are different in the two chapters. In this chapter, the term "client" (all lower case) refers to a computer system that is or can become a managed system of SMS by installation of suitable software (Advanced Client or Legacy Client software). The installation chapter deals with installing Advanced Clients and the term used is "Client" (initial capital).

Although some discovery methods can discover networked systems that are not and cannot become a managed system of SMS, the simplification of discussing "clients" without further qualification is made.

Discovery

> NOTE: The various discovery methods operate on configurable schedules and the discovered information can be used to populate or update relevant collections (see the Collections chapter). However, collections are not automatically updated when the discovery methods are run, but must be updated by running the appropriate query. Update collections before making use of them, as before deploying software based on a collection.

The discovery techniques are

- Network Discovery
- Heartbeat Discovery
- Active Directory Discovery
- Scripted Discovery
- Logon Discovery

Network Discovery

Network Discovery can discover computers and any other type of device attached to the network that is assigned an IP address, such as a router or printer. Network Discovery will only create a DDR for a resource if it can positively determine the resource's subnet mask or Active Directory site. The subnet mask can be determined if:

- The client's IP address is listed in a trusted router's ARP cache, and the router has only a single IP address on that interface.

UNCLASSIFIED

- The client has an SNMP agent running, and network discovery is configured to use the community name the client is configured for.

- The client is a Microsoft DHCP client. This is not an option if you are using advanced security because there is no DHCP support for network discovery in advanced security. If you are using standard security, the SMS site server must have user-level security access on the DHCP servers to retrieve database information from those servers. The SMS Service account must have domain user credentials in the same domain as the DHCP server.

Network Discovery is disabled by default and must be enabled in order for it to operate. To discover computers that are potential SMS clients, configure Network Discovery using its options settings in the SMS Administrator Console. This discovery method can have an adverse effect on network performance; therefore, it is advisable to schedule this task when network activity is low. Network Discovery can also be configured to run on multiple servers using different schedules to reduce the impact on the network. Using Network Discovery may be security relevant in environments where access to the physical network cannot be controlled because it can discover devices that are added to the network without authorization. For such environments, enable Network Discovery. It is important to note that DHCP Network Discovery is not available for advanced security mode. This is by design. Access to DHCP data requires a domain-level account. In advanced security mode, local system accounts are used to access server resources; therefore, DHCP Network Discovery is not an option. See Microsoft's Concepts, Planning, and Deployment Guide [1], Chapter 4, Understanding SMS Clients, and Chapter 17, Discovering Resources and Deploying Clients, for a detailed description of Network Discovery options.

Heartbeat Discovery

Heartbeat Discovery refreshes database discovery data for computers with SMS client software installed. This discovery method is enabled by default and occurs on a preset, configurable schedule. Since having up-to-date data in the database for use by other functions, such as software distribution, is important, do not disable Heartbeat Discovery.

Active Directory Discovery

Directory Discovery is an automatic process that discovers computers, users, user groups, and system groups.

Active Directory System Discovery

The Active Directory System Discovery method polls specified Active Directory containers, such as domains and sites in an Active Directory domain controller, to discover computers. This discovery method can also poll the specified Active Directory containers recursively. Active Directory System Discovery connects to each discovered computer to retrieve details about the computer. The Active Directory domain can be in mixed mode or native mode.

Active Directory User Discovery

The Active Directory User Discovery method polls an Active Directory domain controller to discover users and the user groups of which they are members. This discovery method can also poll the specified Active Directory containers recursively. The Active Directory domain can be in mixed mode or native mode. Containers, such as specific domains, sites, organizational units, or user groups, are specified and SMS routinely polls the containers and, optionally, their child containers for users and their user groups. You can also adjust the schedule of the polling.

UNCLASSIFIED

Active Directory System Group Discovery

The Active Directory System Group Discovery method polls an Active Directory domain controller to discover system groups for computer systems that have been discovered by other discovery methods and assigned to the SMS site. Thus, this discovery method augments the discovery data of other discovery methods. If a resource is not assigned to an SMS site, Active Directory System Group Discovery does not discover system group information for that resource.

Scripted Discovery

Scripts can be developed to create discovery records from a variety of data sources such as spreadsheets, directories, and databases.

Logon Discovery

Clients can be discovered during logon by including discovery scripts as part of logon scripts.

Correlation and Verification

An obvious objective for the SMS administrator is to ascertain that the clients and other systems in the site are those and only those that should be in the site. To this end, crosscheck the information collected by the different discoveries. When multiple discovery methods are used, the discovery results of one type of discovery can be compared to the results of another type. For example, you can create a custom report that compares the results of Network Discovery to Active Directory System Discovery. An LDAP query can be used to validate, at least partially, the findings of an SMS discovery method. Active Directory System Group Discovery provides a degree of correlation by the way it operates.

The expectation is that Active Directory discovery is more reliable and accurate and provides more data than other discovery methods. However, using other methods provides a basis for crosschecking. Network Discovery in particular can provide data that is used by the Active Directory System Group Discovery method.

Regardless of the discovery methods used, administrators should verify that the machines discovered are those and only those that should be on the network by comparing SMS collection information to independent sources of such information, such as an enterprise policy document that includes a network map.

Important Security Points

- ❏ Use SMS Network Discovery if there is risk of unauthorized computers or other devices being attached to the network.
- ❏ Do not disable SMS Heartbeat Discovery, which is enabled by default.
- ❏ Crosscheck the information collected by the different discovery methods.
- ❏ Verify that the machines discovered are those and only those that should be on the network.

SMS Client Installation

This chapter discusses SMS Client installation, covering techniques of installation and relevant security points.

Client Types

There are two types of Clients in SMS 2003: the Advanced Client, new in SMS 2003, and the Legacy Client. The Advanced Client is optimized for mobile and remote use, such as with laptops, and is optimized for possibly low-bandwidth connections. The Advanced Client can be installed only on Windows 2000 and later computers. The Legacy Client is provided for back-level compatibility. This chapter discusses only the Advanced Client.

A **client agent** is software that runs on an SMS client to perform a specific function. All clients in the site run the same set of client agents. Client agents are determined during installation of SMS on a Site Server. Client agents are automatically enabled as appropriate for the functionality that an administrator selects during installation of SMS. The Advanced Client includes all SMS client agents.

Techniques of Installation

Client Push Installation

The Client Push Installation method installs Clients on discovered systems. Once configured, Client Push Installation is fully automatic—no action by the SMS administrator is required. Configuration of the Client Push Installation method involves the following actions and choices:

- Enable Client Push Installation method
- Install Advanced or Legacy Clients

> NOTE: Legacy Client installation is not recommended in an SMS advanced security environment. The Advanced Client uses the local system security context and the computer account of the client to carry out SMS tasks, making it more secure than the SMS Legacy Client.

- Select types of systems to install to—one can choose servers and/or domain controllers and/or workstations; do not install SMS Clients on domain controllers because of a domain controller's critical functionality in Windows domains; as a practical matter, domain controllers will typically be separately administered
- Select the accounts used to do the install

In subsequent discussion, the assumption is that the Clients being installed are Advanced Clients.

UNCLASSIFIED

Client Push Installation installs the Advanced Client software onto computers running Windows 2000, Windows XP, Windows Server 2000, or Windows Server 2003. The account that is used for installation must have administrative privileges on the client. The administrator specifies a list of client accounts when configuring the client push installation method. One or more of the accounts specified must exist on each client computer. During installation, these accounts are tried sequentially until one with appropriate privileges is found. To avoid having to provide a list of accounts that covers all the clients, one can specify "%ComputerName%\AccountName". "AccountName" must exist on all the clients and must have administrative privileges. For "%ComputerName%", SMS substitutes the name of the computer to which the Client is being deployed. This method avoids having to use any accounts with domain privileges.

Client Push Installation Wizard

Client Push installation can also be run manually via the Actions Menu for individual systems or collections. A Client can be installed by selecting the **Install Client Software** option in the SMS Administrative Console regardless of whether Client Push Installation is enabled and regardless of the settings that have been configured. For example, domain controllers may be excluded in the settings but the wizard will install on them if directed to do so.

Group Policy Client Installation

Clients can be installed using the Software Installation options of the Group Policy Object. There are two sections in the Group Policy Object: Computer and User. The software installation section in the Computer section allows software to be installed when a computer boots up. The software installation section in the User section allows the software to be installed when a user logs on to the computer. In the User case, the user has some control over when the software is installed. In the Computer case, the user has no choice in the matter. In either case, the client software must be set up in a .msi file. Either the Legacy Client.msi file can be used or a customized client.msi installation file can be used.

The Group Policy Object is attached to an Active Directory site, domain, or organizational unit. The Client installation in each case will be directed to those computers that are part of the specific site, domain, or organizational unit. An advantage of the group policy method for installation is that it does not require a client software installation account. The key disadvantage is that, by default, no local copy of the source files is created on the client. Local source files are helpful if the client needs to be repaired. A workaround for this is to send the source files to the client via software distribution or with the integrated source path update manager.

If Group Policy Software Installation is used; use a hidden folder for a software distribution point to prevent users from browsing contents of the share point.

Other Installation Techniques

The Advanced Client Installer operates by pulling the Client installation files to a computer and then initiating Client installation. The Advanced Client Installer can be used to install Clients manually from the SMS Administrator Console. It can also be invoked by a logon script at the client. A software distribution package can also invoke the Installer. The package definition script included with SMS 2003 for installing the Advanced Client uses the Advanced Client Installer.

Client Installation Source Files

Client installation source files originate in the primary Site Server SMS directory "\SMS", which contains all the files that SMS installs and is associated with the share SMS_sitecode. The Client installation files are stored in the SMS\Client directory. The SMS Client share is associated with the SMS\Client directory. The SMS\Client directory and the associated SMS Client share also exist on the Management Points. The permissions on these shares give the **Everyone** group **Full Control**. Restrict the permissions on these shares by removing the **Everyone** group and replacing it with the **Authenticated Users** group. The **Authenticated Users** group does not need **Full Control** on these shares. Reduce the permissions of this group to **Read** only.

Important Security Points

- ❏ Install Advanced Client in preference to Legacy Client wherever feasible in your site hierarchy.

- ❏ Do not install SMS Clients on domain controllers.

- ❏ When using Client Push Installation, specify the option to use local administrator accounts for installation on the clients.

- ❏ If Group Policy Software Installation is used; use a hidden folder for a software distribution point to prevent users from browsing contents of the share point.

- ❏ Replace the **Everyone** group with the **Authenticated Users** group in the permissions on the client installation shares—SMS_sitecode share and SMS Client share. Reduce the permissions of this group to **Read** only.

Software Distribution

Software distribution in SMS can be viewed as a general capability to deliver information to a designated set of recipients. As such, its careless or malicious use can cause harm. This chapter examines security issues associated with software distribution and makes recommendations for its secure operation. It begins by reviewing the essentials of software distribution to provide a context for the security discussion.

Overview

As the *SMS 2003 Concepts, Planning and Installation Guide* [1] summarizes, Software Distribution can

- Install software on client computers
- Remove software from client computers
- Copy data files to client computers
- Run utilities on client computers such as virus checks or disk defragmentation
- Distribute packages containing any possible function for execution on a client computer

Figure 4 shows a representation of the SMS software distribution architecture. The dashed green lines are the paths followed by packages; the solid red lines are the paths followed by control information—advertisements, requests for download, and so on.

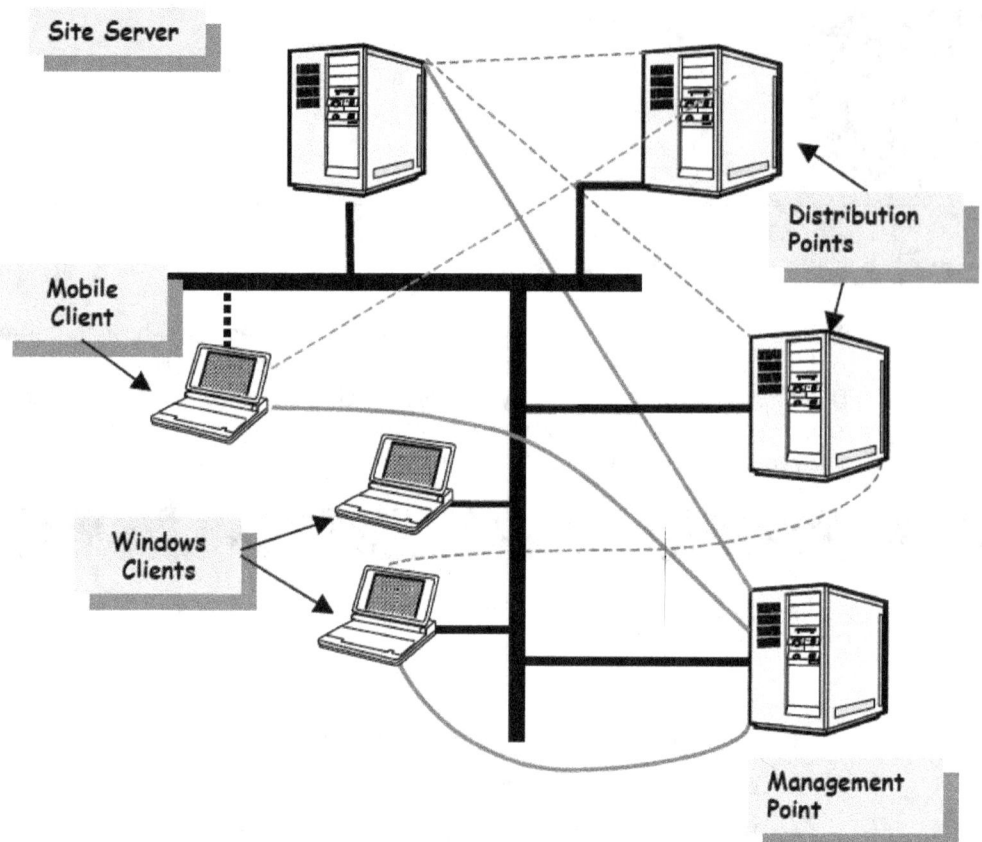

Figure 4. SMS Software Distribution Architecture

Software distribution uses packages as the units of distribution. A *package*, as defined in the *SMS 2003 Concepts, Planning and Installation Guide*, is an object that contains the files and instructions for distributing software to a Distribution Point. Any windows server may act as a *Distribution Point*, as this role simply offers distribution packages either on a windows share or via the Background Intelligent Transfer Service (BITS) protocol. SMS 2003 supports both Legacy and Advanced Clients. The discussion that follows assumes that the SMS server is in advanced security mode and that all the Clients are Advanced Clients.

Software distribution uses advertisements to notify the clients that there is a package available. An *advertisement* is a notification sent by the Site Server to the Management Points specifying that a package is available to clients. The Management Points send the advertisements out to the clients. The clients then contact the Distribution Points in order to obtain and execute the advertised software package. There may be one or more Management Points and/or Distribution Points named for an SMS site for performance and availability reasons. The Site Server is the default Distribution Point and Management Point for the site if no others are specified.

The software distribution package can contain programs, source files, and source file paths. All the elements of a package and their uses are described in the *SMS 2003 Operations Guide*. [3] As noted above, a software distribution package can contain any function. This includes an executable file, an installation script that installs a software application, or simply a command to copy data files.

UNCLASSIFIED

SMS general mechanisms and the Software Distribution capabilities in particular provide an intruder or malicious insider a powerful set of tools for causing mischief. Without proper vigilance and adequate security controls, SMS could be used to spread malicious code—viruses, Trojan horses, corrupt data, or server-fatal command-line shell scripts—that could infect an organization, with the apparent blessing of the organization's administration. Similarly, SMS could be used to enable a vulnerability or Trojan horse that is already on one or more client machines. Thus, it is important to guard SMS Software Distribution operations and related SMS objects as closely as one would guard a Domain Administrator's account.

Any primary Site Server in the SMS Site hierarchy can initiate a software distribution process. A malicious individual could potentially distribute a wide variety of malicious applications via software distribution. Thus, restrict access to the primary Site Server to those who are trusted and need to have access to it.

Setting up SMS Systems for Distribution

This section considers security in setting up the systems or components involved in software distribution. The discussion covers the following topics:

- Primary Site Servers
- Distribution Points
- Management Points
- Advertised Programs Client Agent
- Original Source File Location

Primary Site Servers

As depicted by the sample site hierarchy in Figure 5, each primary site has a Site Server with an associated SQL database and an SMS Administrator Console. Each primary Site Server can affect the systems at its site as well as those at its child sites. The central site has the maximum span of influence in the SMS site hierarchy. Thus, it also has the greatest potential to propagate errors in the software distribution process. Obviously, a malicious user in control of the server at the central site has great potential to cause harm. Thus, the security rights and object permissions at the central site may deserve the special attention of the administrator. Since the central site is the repository for all information gathered from the entire site hierarchy, the administrator may also need to take special precautions to protect the associated SQL server database. Clearly, the same admonitions apply to all primary sites but the degree of risk may vary and it is the latter that administrators must assess.

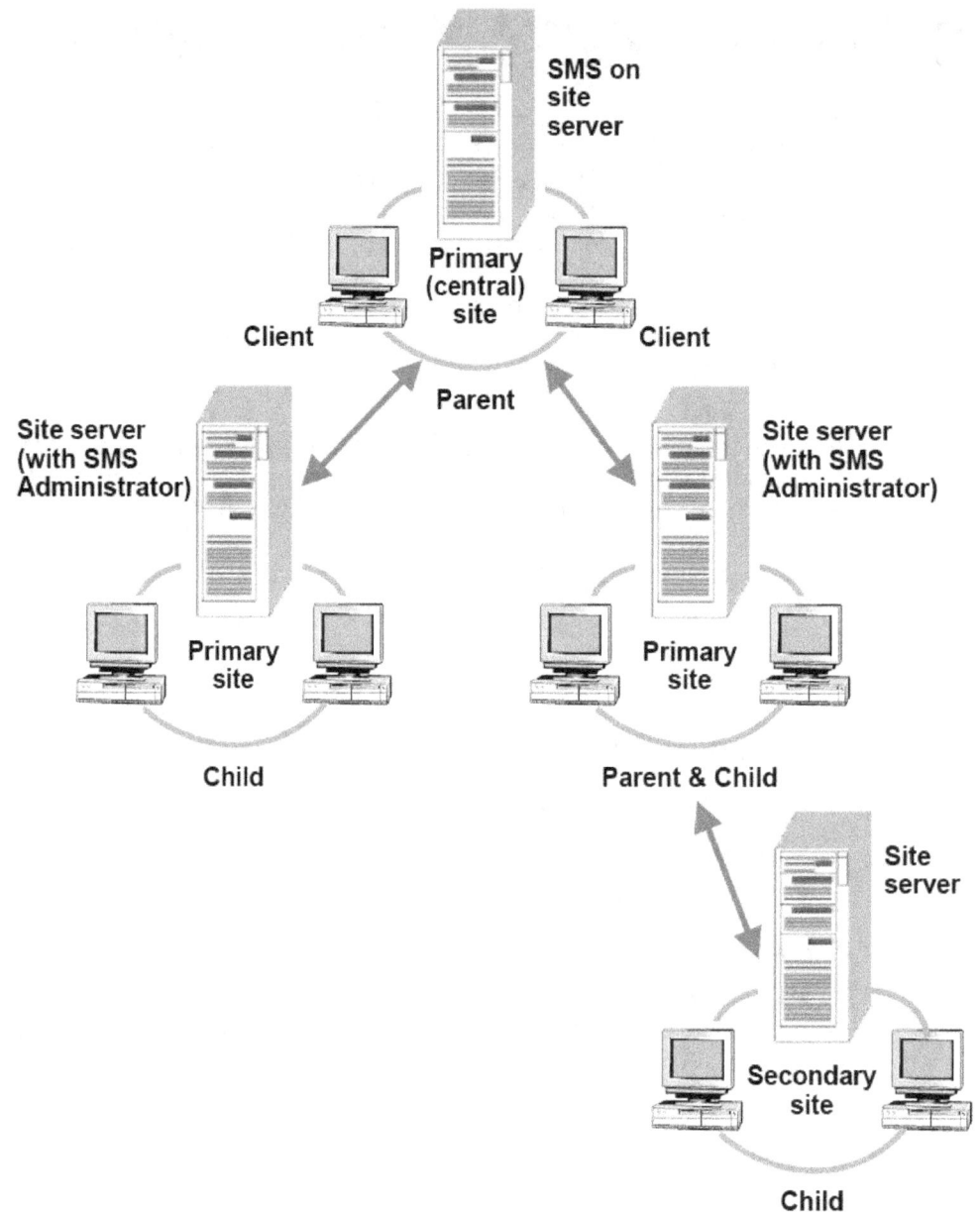

Figure 5. An Example of an SMS Site Hierarchy

Distribution Points

A Distribution Point stores packages received from a Site Server. These packages contain compressed copies of the source files if the **Use a compressed copy of the source directory** option was chosen when the package was created at the Site Server. If instead, the **Always obtain files from the source directory** option was chosen, the package stored at the Distribution Point contains uncompressed source files[6]. Later, when the client responds to an advertisement by requesting the associated package from the Distribution Point, the Distribution Point sends the package to the client.

---

[6]   The compression algorithm is the same proprietary algorithm used for compressing data sent from the advanced clients to the Management Points.

UNCLASSIFIED

To ensure the integrity of packages downloaded to Advanced Clients, SMS calculates and signs hash values for packages when they are sent from the originating site to Distribution Points and child sites. SMS automatically includes the hash values in advertisements of those packages. Then, when a package is downloaded, clients verify that the hash value of the package matches the hash value of the advertised program before running the advertised program. Note that the hash is checked only when the package is downloaded, not when it is run from a Distribution Point. Since this hash check helps to ensure the integrity of the content and that the correct software is installed, use the download method for installation when creating the corresponding advertisement. The only apparent disadvantage to the download method is that the package files are stored in a cache that users have access to. This is discussed later in the subsection **Distributing the Package**.

Package File Access on Distribution Points

The share that contains the packages on the Distribution Point is given the share name *computername*\SMSPKG*driveletter*$ on the NTFS drive that contains the most available space. The default share permissions give **Full Access** on this share to **Everyone**. For better security, delete the **Everyone** group and add the **Authenticated Users** group with **Read** permission on the share. Each package is stored in a separate folder that is identified by the package ID number. The default package access permissions allow Users and Guests **Read, Read & Execute, and List Folder Contents** permissions and Administrators **Full Control** permissions to the package files on Distribution Points that hold the packages. If not all users require access to the packages in a folder; modify the access permissions on that folder to specify the least permissions required.

Access to these files can be further restricted by defining package access accounts. There are two default generic accounts that are defined: an Administrator's account with **Full Control** that is mapped to the local Administrators group and a User's account with **Read** access that is mapped to the local Users group. In addition to these default accounts, a specific Windows User Access Account or a new generic access account can be added with specific rights. Right click **Access Accounts** under a package in the **Packages** folder in the SMS Administrator Console and click the menu item **New**.... The pop-up menu provides a choice between generic access account and a windows user access account. The generic account can be for Users, Guests, or Administrators. The access permissions (**Read, Change, Full Control**, or **No Access**) can be specified for either type of account. Any changes to the package access accounts should be made at the time of package creation. Changes made to a package after it exists on the Distribution Point requires a refresh of the package.

Management Points

A Management Point (MP) is a site system having the Management Point role. An MP provides a communication point between a Site Server and Advanced Clients. An MP has advertisements for packages and sends these to specified[7] clients. Access to the MP files needs to be limited to the SMS accounts involved in distribution and to a restricted number of administrators. Unauthorized access to the advertisement information could cause denial of service when a client attempts to download or install the advertised package.

Advertised Programs Client Agent

The Advertised Programs client agent controls the way in which clients check for advertised programs and the way they behave when an advertised program is available. Setup for Advertised Programs client agents is done in the SMS Administrator's Console

---

[7] The clients are specified in a target collection, which is discussed later.

(properties of the **Client Agents** folder in the **Site Settings** folder). If the administrator selects **Enable software distribution to clients**, the Advertised Programs client agents is installed on all Legacy Client computers within the site, and SMS enables the Advertised Programs client agent on all Advanced Client computers within the site. If the **Enable software distribution to clients** box is not checked, clients cannot use SMS to install or run software, including software updates. The administrator also sets other properties of the client, such as:

- Interval for client to check for new advertised programs
- Whether to display new program notification messages

It follows that access to the Client Agents folder would enable a malicious or careless user to disrupt software distribution operations. Thus, limit access to the Client Agents folder on the SMS Administrator's Console to those authorized to turn on or to turn off software distribution for the site. Restricting access to specific folders can be accomplished with custom consoles, as described in *Chapter 6, SMS Administrator Console.*

Original Source File Location

Packages that have *package source files*[8] obtain those source files from one of several locations, depending on the option chosen when the package was created and the reason the package is obtaining the source files. As mentioned earlier, there are two settings for obtaining source files when creating a package: **Use a compressed copy of the source directory** and **Always obtain files from the source directory**. For this discussion, these options will be referred to as "compressed" and "uncompressed," respectively. The three actions that cause distribution of package source files are

- Creation—when a package is created

- Refresh—when software files at the Distribution Point are replaced because they are corrupted

- Update—when a source file has been changed

Table 3 contains a listing of where the source files come from and how they are stored in each of these situations.

Table 3. Source File Location

Distribution Scope	Owner Site Source File Setting	Action	Result
Distribution only within site	Compressed	Creation	The compressed file is stored as a *.pkg file on the Site Server.
Distribution includes child sites	Compressed	Creation	A compressed copy of the package is sent to each child site having Distribution Points for the package.
Distribution only within site	Uncompressed	Creation	The package source files are copied from the source to the Distribution Point of the site.
Distribution includes child sites	Uncompressed	Creation	A compressed copy of the package is created and stored as a *.pck file. The compressed copy is sent to each child site having Distribution Points for the package.

---

[8] Recall that a package could consist of just a command line with no additional files required.

UNCLASSIFIED

Distribution only within site	Compressed	Refresh	The compressed *.pkg file is decompressed to the Distribution Point.
Distribution includes child sites	Compressed	Refresh	The child site owning the Distribution Point decompresses the compressed copy on the Site Server to the Distribution Point.
Distribution only within site	Uncompressed	Refresh	The source is copied to the Distribution Point.
Distribution includes child sites	Uncompressed	Refresh	The child site owning the Distribution Point decompresses the compressed copy on the child Site Server to the Distribution Point.
Distribution only within site	Compressed	Update	The updated package source directory is compressed again, overwriting the existing *.pkg file.
Distribution includes child sites	Compressed	Update	The package source is recompressed and stored as a *.pck file. The compressed file is sent to the child sites where Distribution Points are present.
Distribution only within site	Uncompressed	Update	The package source is copied from the source directory to the Distribution Point. No compression occurs.
Distribution includes child sites	Uncompressed	Update	The package source is compressed and stored as a *.pck file. The compressed file is sent to the child sites where Distribution Points are present.

It is critical that the locations where the source files are stored, whether in a compressed or uncompressed form, be protected to prevent an attacker from getting access to the source files and disrupting software distribution.

Setting up Software for Distribution

This section explores security concerns related to creation, distribution, and installation of a package by SMS.

General Mechanisms

There are two mechanisms that are helpful in managing SMS software distribution security: SMS object security (discussed in *Chapter 5: Objects, Permissions, and Accounts*) and Windows 2000 permissions, including file and active directory permissions. The former allows control of *packages*, *advertisements*, *sites*, and *collections* through the SMS Administrator Console; it is critical in ensuring the integrity of software distribution control. The latter enables access control of critical SMS software distribution components as well as separation of duties through implementation of roles. For more information, refer to the *SMS 2003 Operations Guide.* [3]

Preparing for Package Creation

The integrity of source files and the SMS package for installing them supports the integrity and security of the entire SMS operation. Loss of integrity negatively affects the SMS operation. Whatever the choice of installation utility used by the internal or the external publisher of the software, in your role as SMS administrator, require a means for authenticating the origin and the integrity of the sources. Examples include publisher certificates, digital signature, or signed hash value checking before installation.

Before creating the SMS package, carefully pick the location for storing the source files. Select a path that is on a machine or share dedicated for SMS use, or on a machine or share with access limited to SMS and a select few administrators. In addition, review and test the software that will be offered for distribution.

Creating the Package

The administrator can use the package tools from the SMS Administrator's Console to do one of the following:

- Use a package definition file[9] supplied with the sources by the vendor

- Create a new package definition and package from scratch

The administrator must have object permissions that include *administer* a package, and permissions to create, delete, and modify an advertisement. In your role as administrator, test the SMS packages that will be advertised.

When creating packages, turn on the checkbox **Disconnect users from distribution points**. Failure to check this box means that SMS may not be able to update the package, which is a denial of service. In addition, there is the problem that users might get part of the old version of the package and part of the new version, which would cause the install to fail.

When creating the program for the package, on the Environment tab of the Program properties window are two options: **Run with user rights** and **Run with administrative rights**. Select **Run with user rights** unless the package requires administrative rights. If administrative rights are needed, use the option to install only when no user is logged on. If you must run the install with administrative rights and when a user is logged on, do not allow the user to interact with the program. However, if the program requires user interaction in order to run, this clearly will not work. In this case, try to find an alternate program for the install that does not require user interaction. Failing that, consider other measures, such as having an administrator take the place of the usual user for the install. The extent to which you need to be concerned here obviously depends on the extent to which you trust the user to behave in accord with enterprise policy. The important point is to avoid running something with administrative rights when a user is logged in and can interact with the program.

Distributing the Package

Administrators doing package distribution can use existing collections or can define new collections of targets for packages. A collection of targets is a set of client computers in a site defined by membership rules. In formulating your organization's policy, limit the number of administrators who can create new collections in order to reduce the impact of accidental or malicious universal distributions of badly behaved software. Similarly, as SMS administrator, limit the number of people with security permissions to modify or create advertisements to reduce the risk of erroneous or malicious advertisements.

> WARNING: Microsoft document reference [11] offers the following admonition. Any administrator who can link their collection to a collection of targets can cause their collection to receive the advertisements targeted to the other collection, even when they do not have Advertise permissions on any collection. For this reason, watch for the addition of subcollections to collections with advertisements, and be cautious about whom you give permission to read collections that receive advertisements.

---

[9] A package definition file is a specially formatted file describing a package and one or more programs.

UNCLASSIFIED

Recent Windows platforms add further assistance through the Windows policies on *Software Restrictions*. These policies are currently available only for Windows XP and Windows 2003 servers. They enable a client to check installs against certificates in certain install environments at the operating system level. This offers additional client-side protection against distribution and reception of a malicious package.

Since Advanced Clients use a download cache, in which advertised programs are stored until run, it is important to provide operating system security hardening [10] for client machines to protect the integrity of the download cache. By default, only privileged users have access to the cache location. However, SMS can be configured to allow users to modify this location. If the location is modified, ensure permissions on the new directory location are limited to only those users requiring access. Once a package has been installed, delete it from the cache as a general security precaution since anyone with access to the cache can run the package. This will ensure that sensitive or restricted information is not exposed. Authorized users have two options for deleting items in the cache: (1) if configured, the System Management icon on the client allows the user to see the cache folder and makes available the option to empty the cache; (2) if appropriate directory permissions are granted, the user can use Windows Explorer to navigate to the cache folder and selectively delete files.

> WARNING: All users have read and execute privileges on the default cache location. Realize, if the software is downloaded, this allows the user to copy the file to a directory or shared folder that can be accessed by other users. Unless absolutely necessary, do not configure SMS to allow users to modify the cache location.

Delta Replication

When changes are made to existing software packages, only the specific files that are new or have changed are propagated by the SMS Site Servers to Distribution Points, not the entire package. To ensure that the package not only works but also does not degrade security, test the modified package before distributing it.

Mobile Support

When Advanced Clients connect remotely, they use BITS, which automatically detects network connection capacity and adjusts the rate of downloading dynamically so other services using the network link are not impacted. If the client disconnects from the network while downloading a package, the download will continue where it left off when the client reconnects. BITS's assumption that client disconnects are normal introduces the possibility of a man-in-the-middle attack[11] on that client. This possibility can be mitigated by using a Virtual Private Network.

Courier Sender

Courier Sender is an SMS function that enables software to be sent between SMS sites via CD-ROM or other media. This feature can be useful in situations where available network bandwidth is too low to send packages from site to site or from site to Distribution Point. To ensure the integrity of the CD or other media, allow only trusted individuals to handle its creation, transportation, and distribution using a procedure that

---

[10]   See the NSA Security Guides for Windows platforms.
[11]   A man-in-the-middle attack is one in which the attacker interposes himself or herself between two communicating parties and both intercepts and relays information between the parties. By executing this deception, the attacker convinces both parties that they are talking directly to the other when in fact they are communicating through the attacker.

enables them to maintain control of the media and its contents. Digital signatures can be used to ensure the data has not been changed in transit.

Advertisements and Old Software

When an advertisement is disabled, the formerly advertised package is no longer displayed as being available. However, any source files referenced by the formerly advertised package remain intact in their current storage locations. Thus, even though a package is no longer available, source files referenced by the package may still be downloadable by a client. For example, suppose an old version of a tool with some security problems has been replaced by a newer version and the administrator has disabled the advertisements associated with the old version. The old tool will not be available via SMS but it may still be available to download by other means. To avoid problems, remove old software from the system, do not just disable it.

Security Protection through Roles

The general principle to apply here is the partitioning of a process into roles, each role having only the permissions required to do the assigned portion of the process. There are many ways to define roles in the software distribution area. One partitioning can be achieved by considering the previously identified steps in software distribution as roles assigned to administrative staff.

The three functions noted for setting up distribution of a package—software acquisition, package definition and creation, and package distribution—partition the effort into three roles[12] as shown in. Table 4 identifies the essential tasks for each role. Note that some SMS functions may be considered for more than one phase and may vary depending on the organization's specific needs.

Table 4. Sample Roles for Software Distribution

	Software Acquisition	SMS Package Definition	SMS Package Distribution
Purpose	Pick and test software to be distributed	Prepare the software for distribution by SMS	Enable and perform the SMS distribution operation
Key Tasks	Prepare software installation files	Create package from sources or *package source files*	Define who gets the distribution, when, and how
	Verify integrity of files to be distributed	Test resulting package and rework distribution packages that fail	Define whether mandatory or optional
	Place source files in path location for SMS actions	Remove package when no longer active	Define/modify the advertisements

---

[12]   These phases are an arbitrary but logical division of the process solely for this discussion. Other partitioning of tasks into roles is possible; the one discussed here is just one example. Assignment of roles will depend, in specific cases, on organization structure and size, size and technical depth of administrative staff, SMS site hierarchy, and so on. For example, a specific maintenance role might be useful for some organizations, although its function can generally be partitioned among the three roles defined here.

UNCLASSIFIED

	Software Acquisition	SMS Package Definition	SMS Package Distribution
	Check/supply authentication certificates/hashes as possible	Monitor/manage the definition process	Monitor/manage the distribution process, reporting distribution failures as appropriate

Table 5 shows the assignment of permissions on objects for each role.

Table 5. Object Class Permissions for Sample Roles

SMS Object/Function	Software Acquisition	SMS Package Definition	SMS Package Distribution
Source Directory	Full Control	Read Only	None
SMS Administrator Console	None	Read, Execute	Read, Execute
Packages	None	Administer	Read
Collections	None	None	Advertise, Administer
Advertisements	None	None	Administer
Sites	None	None	Read
Status Messages	None	None	Read

NOTE: All other users or groups, outside of SMS Admins, should have "no access." This table does not address permissions needed for other SMS functions.

Software Acquisition

Whatever the source of the software, the group or individual with the role to approve selections for SMS distribution

- Verifies that the external software publisher (or the internal department publisher) is reputable and that the installation files and instructions actually come from that publisher
- Requires of the publisher a means for authenticating the origin and the integrity of the sources, such as a signed hash value, digital signature, or digital certificate
- Performs virus scanning and other testing on software and installation kits

The person in this role places an approved, verified, digitally signed installation bundle in a protected network location for package source files. This role has Administer permission for the source file location but needs no other permissions associated with SMS. No other function needs more than read access to this location. General domain users do not need access to this location.

SMS Package Definition

The role responsible for SMS package definition accepts only those submissions that have passed through Software Acquisition to ensure the integrity of the source files.

Since this role creates packages, making them available for distribution, it is assigned the permissions needed to administer the package object, but not to distribute it. For example, this role has no need to access collections since collections are used to define the target of a distribution and do not affect the package itself.[13]

For maximum integrity, give the Administer permission for packages only to those persons directly associated with the package-definition role; assign everyone else **Read** permission at most. Conversely, those involved with package definition need little access to any other SMS function.

SMS Package Distribution

Since this role distributes packages, it needs the permissions necessary to effect the distribution to a selection of users and computers and to monitor its progress.

Do not give this role any rights to create new SMS packages or to modify old packages. This offers security protection against an intruder, since an intruder must gain access to both the Package Definition and Distribution roles to have the permissions needed to distribute other than an approved package with the right digital signature. Similarly, an insider responsible for performing the distribution role cannot distribute an untried set of software.

Important Security Points

- ❑ Limit access to the primary Site Server to those who are trusted and require the access. Give special attention to the security rights and object permissions at the central site and take necessary precautions to protect the associated SQL server database.

- ❑ Use the download method for package installation.

- ❑ Remove the **Everyone** group and add the **Authenticated Users** group for the Distribution Point package share. Grant the **Authenticated Users** group read access to the share.

- ❑ If not all users require access to a package, modify the access permissions to specify the least permissions.

- ❑ Define package access accounts.

- ❑ Limit access for Management Point advertisements to the SMS accounts involved in distribution and to a restricted number of administrators.

- ❑ Limit access to the Client Agents folder on the SMS Administrator Console to those authorized to turn on or to turn off software distribution for the site.

- ❑ Protect locations where source files are stored, whether in compressed or uncompressed form.

- ❑ Require an authentication means for source files, such as publisher certificates, digital signature, or hash value checking.

- ❑ Put the source files on a machine or share used only by SMS, or on a machine or share where only SMS and a select few administrators have access.

- ❑ Review and test the software that will be offered for distribution and test the SMS packages that will be advertised.

---

[13] This view, in which the Software Package Definition role has no access to Collections, is a simplified way to describe the role. In practice, the person creating the package may need to know the types of systems receiving the data and hence may need to characterize the possible targets. This implies access to inventory data; hence, practical considerations could give this role access to other objects and operations.

UNCLASSIFIED

- When creating packages, turn on the checkbox **Disconnect users from Distribution Points**.

- When creating a program for a package, select the option to run with User rights unless the package requires administrative rights.

- If administrative rights are needed for running a package's program, use the option to install **Only when no user is logged on**.

- Avoid running a package program with administrative rights when a user is logged in and can interact with the program.

- Once a package has been installed, delete it from the download cache.

- Limit the number of administrators who can create new collections of targets.

- Limit security permissions for modifying and creating advertisements.

- When available, use Windows policies on *Software Restrictions* to allow clients to check installs against certificates.

- Provide security protection for client machines to protect the integrity of the download cache.

- Test modified packages before distributing them.

- Use a Virtual Private Network to mitigate the possibility of a man-in-the-middle attack on a client connecting remotely.

- Allow only trusted individuals to create, transport, and distribute material created by the Courier Sender process and ensure that they use a procedure that enables them to maintain control of the media and its contents.

- Remove old software from the system; do not just disable its advertisement.

- Partition the software distribution process into roles, each role having only the permissions required for the assigned portion of the process.

    - Give the software-acquisition role Administer permission for the source file location but no other permissions associated with SMS.

    - Give the package-definition role Administer permission for packages; give everyone else only **Read** permission.

    - Give the package-distribution role the permissions necessary to effect distribution to a selection of users and computers and to monitor distribution progress but not rights to create new SMS packages or to modify old packages.

Software Metering

SMS Software Metering is a tool within SMS that enables monitoring of software running on computers within the SMS site. It can be configured to detect and report the use of all or selected computer programs within the SMS site, and can be used to ensure that selected software is being used within the bounds of licensing agreements. Software Metering can be used to help enforce security policies within SMS.

As with other tools within SMS, secure configuration is important to Software Metering usage. For example, if an unauthorized user changes Software Metering rules, use of an undesirable executable will not be recorded and domain security measures may be undermined. It is important to consider the various security options available and to implement basic security protections. This chapter discusses the basic principles of SMS Software Metering and recommends security configuration protections.

Overview of Operation and Configuration

Software Metering security begins with a basic understanding of Software Metering usage and its components. Software Metering monitors and collects usage data on selected executables running on SMS clients. Software Metering components are the Software Metering server, Management Points, and client agents. Software Metering can be performed on clients running the Legacy Client, the Advanced Client, or Terminal Services.

The Software Metering server is a process that runs on the SMS Site Server. The Management Points provide communication between the Site Server and the Software Metering Client Agents that reside on client computers. All SMS communication between the Site Server and the clients is done via the Management Point.

Configure Software Metering by defining Software Metering rules. Software Metering rules are configured by an administrator in the SMS Administrator Console and are stored in the SMS site database. These rules identify software that must be monitored. Each rule specifies a product name, an executable file name, version, and language. For example, the administrator might specify that Internet Explorer should be monitored. The administrator might enter "Microsoft Internet Explorer" as the product name, "iexplore.exe" as the executable file name, 6.00.2600.0000 as the version, and "English (United States)" as the language. The effect of creating such a rule is described later in this chapter under Operation.

Rules are passed to the Management Points. The Software Metering Client Agent downloads the Software Metering rules from a Management Point. The Software Metering Client Agent performs the metering activities and the metering data is sent to the Site Server via the Management Point. The Site Server processes the data and stores it in the site database. This process is shown in Figure 6 below.

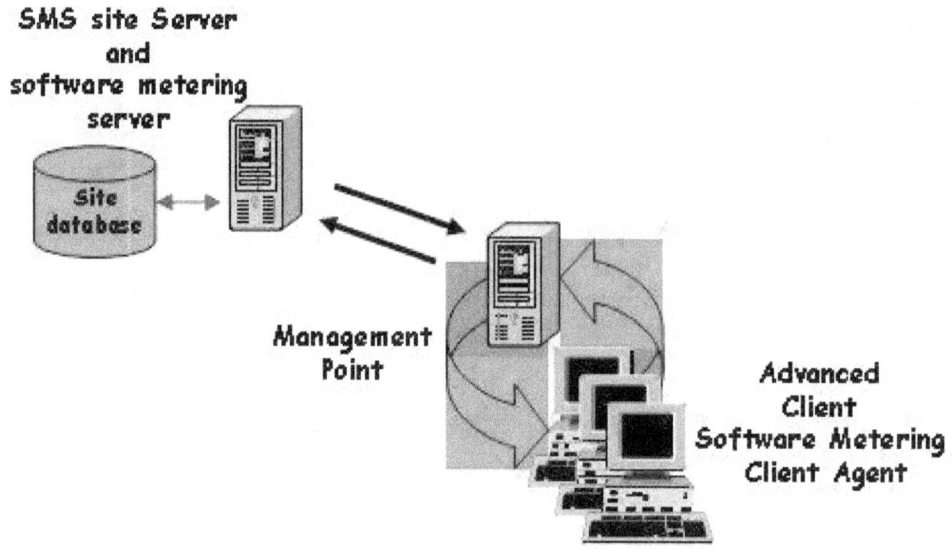

Figure 6. Overview of Software Metering Components

Software Metering in this version of SMS does not perform on-line software licensing. Previous versions of this product could be used to distribute software licenses on an as-needed basis, but the feature was not included in this version of SMS.

Installation

Software Metering server components are installed when SMS is installed on the SMS Site Server. Installation of the Software Metering Client Agent occurs automatically on a client during Advanced Client installation. The client components are enabled from the Client Agents folder of the site settings folder.

Configuration, Operation, and Reporting

Server Configuration

Software Metering is enabled on the SMS Site Server by configuring appropriate Software Metering rules. These rules are configured through the Software Metering Rules icon contained in the SMS Administrator Console. It is recommended that a specific Software Metering administrator account be created to provide control over the creation, modification, and deletion of metering rules and activities.

Software Metering rules are configured for monitoring single software programs. A Software Metering rule specifies information about the program and how the rule is to be applied. Each rule specifies product name, program name, version, language, SMS site code, and SMS object security rights. An important rule specification is the setting of object security rights. These include the Class security rights and Instance security rights associated with the Software Metering rule. The name of the Security Class is Software Metering Rule and the Security Instance refers to a particular Software Metering rule. The rights that can be set are Administer, Create, Delegate, Delete, Modify, and Read. These rights can be set per rule per user if that level of granularity is desired. The site code applies the specific rule to a specific SMS site. Child site inheritance can only be specified at the time of rule creation. Because of this, use care when setting inheritance

UNCLASSIFIED

for metering rules. Inheritance could change which metering rules are applied within a multi-tiered site.

Client Configuration

The Software Metering Client Agent is configured from the Software Metering Client Agent properties contained in the Client Agents folder of the SMS Administrator Console. The client agent is enabled from the General tab of the Software Metering client agent Properties. The client agent configuration applies to the entire SMS site. The data collection schedule and the rule download schedule are configured from the client agent configuration for the Legacy Client. The download schedule for the Advanced Client is set using the Schedule tab of the Software Metering Client Agent Properties.

Operation

Software Metering monitors and records software usage in accordance with administrator-specified rules. As shown previously in Figure 6, the SMS Site Server performs the Software Metering rule configuration. These Software Metering rules are distributed to the communication points, which then distribute the rules to the Software Metering Client Agent within the site. The client agent receives and implements the metering rules for program usage on the client.

The Software Metering Client Agent examines each program that runs on the client and determines whether the program matches a rule specified for the client. When a metered program runs on a client, the program information, including start time and end time of the program, is stored on the client. Data collection from the client to the server occurs at scheduled intervals that are set through the client agent configuration.

In a multi-tiered SMS hierarchy, it is possible to apply metering rules to a selected site or to apply rules to children of the SMS site system where the rules are being managed. This is possible only at rule creation time. After assigning a rule to one or more SMS sites, the rule cannot be modified. To change an existing rule, it must be deleted and a new rule must be created.

A child site receives and applies Software Metering rule additions, updates, and deletions from its parent site whenever a rule is created or changed. In addition, each site in the hierarchy can have it's own Software Metering rules. If a site has the Software Metering Client Agent disabled, it still sends rules received from the SMS parent site to lower level sites, as shown in Figure 7.

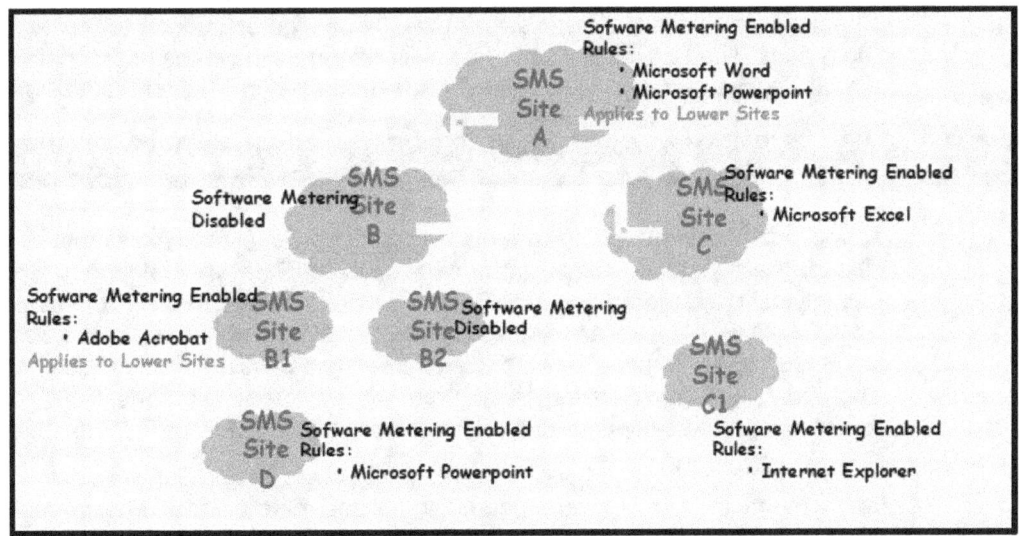

Figure 7. Software Metering in an SMS Hierarchy

Reviewing the SMS hierarchy along with the Software Metering rules shown, the rules that apply at each site are listed in Table 6. Data is collected from clients within these sites based on the metering rule application shown.

Table 6. Software Metering Rule Application

Site Name	Software Metering Rule Application
A	Microsoft Word®, Microsoft PowerPoint®
B	Disabled
B1	Microsoft Word, Microsoft PowerPoint, Adobe® Acrobat®
B2	Disabled
C	Microsoft Word, Microsoft PowerPoint, Microsoft Excel®
C1	Microsoft Word, Microsoft PowerPoint, Internet Explorer®
D	Microsoft Word, Microsoft PowerPoint, Adobe Acrobat

Over time, program usage data is collected on each client. In accord with the set schedule, the collected program usage data is forwarded from the client to the Management Point. From the Management Point, the data is sent to the SMS Site Server and stored in the SMS site database. The data that is stored in the site database is summarized in order to reduce the amount of space it occupies. The data is condensed and old data is deleted. After the data is collected, summarized, and stored in the site database, the SMS reporting function is used to view the data from the SMS Administrator Console.

Reporting

The Software Metering Reporting function is used to review the data that has been collected from the site clients. Software Metering predefined reports are available and custom Software Metering reports can be created. The reporting function is discussed in Chapter 13 of this guide. Permissions must be configured in order to create, view, and run reports. The Software Metering administrator must have the appropriate permissions on the Reports security object class. This is discussed in Chapter 5 of this guide.

Security

Unauthorized use of the Software Metering process, data, and tools must be prevented. The Software Metering administrator must have the Software Metering rule object security right. In order to apply the Software Metering rules to a site, the administrator must have the Meter instance right. The Meter instance right is set at the **Security Tab** of the **Site Properties** page. The Software Metering administrator must also have the appropriate security rights for viewing, running, and creating reports. Refer to Chapter 5 for information on setting security rights and permissions for the Reports object class.

Access control should be used to restrict the permissions on Software Metering folders and files that contain Software Metering rules and metered data. Management Points temporarily store metering rules and data and facilitate their exchange between the SMS

UNCLASSIFIED

Site Server and the SMS clients. Verify that permissions on Software Metering folders and files that contain Software Metering rules and information have not been changed from their default settings. Default permissions permit System and Administrators full control. The default metering folders are \SMS\inboxes\swmproc.box\ and its subfolders on the Site Server. Also, verify the permissions on the file meterRules.mrx that is contained in the subfolder \SMS\inboxes\swmproc.box\rules\ on the Site Server. An unauthorized user accessing this file could modify metering usage data or make other changes to cause a denial of service.

A Software Metering rule specifies several pieces of information about the program that is to be monitored. Each metering rule specifies product name, program name (executable program name), version, language, SMS site code, and SMS object security rights.

Take care when specifying executable programs because some programs function as placeholders for other executables. Make sure that the Software Metering rule specifies the executable that ultimately runs as a process when the program is executed on the client. For example, executing pbrush.exe on Windows XP clients results in the mspaint.exe process. A rule specifying pbrush.exe as the filename/original filename would have no effect on Windows XP clients. The process name is part of the header information for the executable. Software Metering is designed to match the header information of the executable when original filename is specified so that modifying the filename will not circumvent Software Metering. Keep in mind; if filename is specified and the original filename is left blank when creating the rule, modifying the name of the executable would circumvent Software Metering. Ensure the original filename is specified when creating Software Metering rules. A metering rule specifying mspaint.exe as the original filename successfully monitors the user's execution of pbrush.exe. Note also that the version information must match the header information in the executable. If you do not want to specify the version information, you need to put in a wildcard character. Leaving the version information blank will only match a blank version in the header information.

Auditing provides a record of Software Metering events and actions. The SMS Administrator Console contains a System Status folder, which contains site status data in the Site Status subfolder. The status of the Software Metering Processor is recorded in the Component status folder of the Site Status folder. Periodically review this status information for error messages to ensure that the metering process is being performed without errors. In addition, enable the logging feature for the Software Metering Processor by running the SMS Service Manager, which is found in the Tools menu of the SMS Administrator Console. Review the log file for the Software Metering Processor to ensure that the metering process is being performed appropriately. Review the Software Metering rules, configurations, and lists against site policy periodically by running Reports of Software Metering or running customized metering reports.

Important Security Points

- [ ] Give the account that does Software Metering the Software Metering rule object security right and the Meter instance right.
- [ ] Verify permissions are the most restrictive if changed from their default settings.
- [ ] Take care to ensure that the named executable and version information are correct when specifying executable programs in Software Metering rules.
- [ ] Periodically review the status information of the Software Metering Processor to discover error messages.
- [ ] Enable logging of the Software Metering Processor.
- [ ] Periodically review the log file for the Software Metering Processor.
- [ ] Periodically review the Software Metering rules, configurations, and lists against site policy by running reports of Software Metering or running customized metering reports.

UNCLASSIFIED

Remote Tools

System Management Server 2003 includes a suite of remote tools and services that enable direct control and monitoring of client systems. These tools and services enable an authorized SMS user to operate, troubleshoot, and diagnose clients that are connected via a network. The SMS remote toolbox includes remote control, remote reboot, remote chat, remote file transfer, remote execute, SMS client diagnostics, and ping test. SMS 2003 Remote Tools consists of a client agent and a server side tool that work together via a network.

Also accessible in SMS 2003 are two remote services features that are offered by the underlying operating system: Remote Assistance and Terminal Services.

Secure configuration is essential to Remote Tools usage. An administrator remotely accessing a client machine has many rights and it is possible for the administrator to have a remote control session without the knowledge of the client user. It is important to consider the various security options available and to implement basic security protections.

This chapter discusses the basic principles of SMS Remote Tools and their security options and recommends security protections.

Overview

Secure configuration of Remote Tools begins with an understanding of tool implementation and functionality. The remote toolbox provides authorized users remote access to a client machine from an SMS 2003 server. The toolbox and its components are shown below in Figure 8.

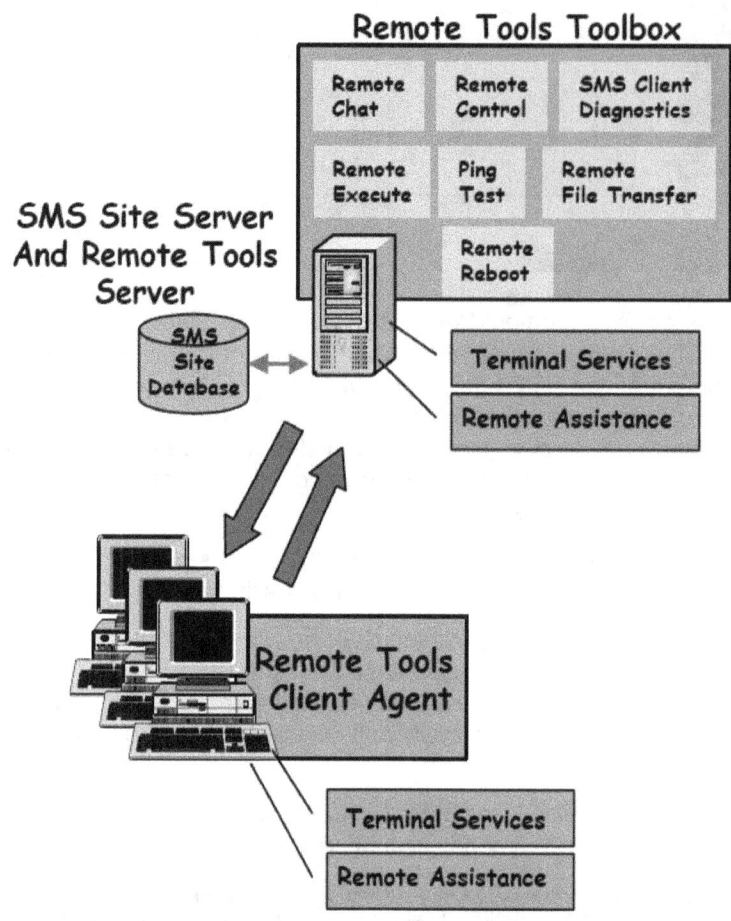

Figure 8. Remote Tools Components

Remote Tools consists of a Remote Tools server-side component along with a Remote Tools client agent that resides on the client systems. The server-side component is responsible for setting the initial client agent configuration and for initiating and controlling the remote control session.

The server-side component contains the toolbox of operation-specific tools. This includes remote chat, remote control, SMS client diagnostics, remote execute, remote file transfer, ping test, and remote reboot.

Table 7 briefly describes these tools.

Table 7. Remote Tools Components

Tool Name	Function
Remote Chat	Remote Chat enables chat between a user on an SMS server and a user on an SMS client. Remote Chat must be initiated on the server.
Remote Control	Remote Control is used on both the client and the server. On the server, Remote Control enables remote viewing and manipulation of the client desktop. On the client, Remote Control allows a user to specify remote control permissions and notification options.

60

Tool Name	Function
SMS Client Diagnostics	SMS Client Diagnostics is used on the server to troubleshoot client hardware and software problems.
Remote Execute	Remote Execute is used on the server to run an application or a batch file on a client.
Remote File Transfer	Remote File Transfer is used on the server to transfer files between the server and a client.
Ping Test	Ping Test is used on the server to test client connectivity on the network.
Remote Reboot	Remote Reboot is used on the server to restart a client.

The Remote Tools client agent controls the remote tool applications running on the client computer. It is initially configured by the server-side component.

Installation

Remote Tools components can be installed on the SMS Site Server during installation. The client agent installation occurs automatically to all site clients when the Remote Tools client agent is enabled on the server.

Configuration

Server

The Remote Tools client agent must be configured for the SMS site before using the tools. This agent can be configured and activated by accessing the Remote Tool Client Agent Properties available under the Site Settings folder in the SMS Administrator Console.

The client agent properties are divided into five categories accessible through corresponding tabs in the Remote Tools Client Agent Properties

- General
- Security
- Policy
- Notification
- Advanced

The General properties enable the client agent and allow the administrator to indicate whether the clients can change the administrator's settings in the Policy and Notification properties. By default, the clients are not allowed to change the Policy and Notification properties. This page also contains the Remote Assistance settings. These settings allow the administrator to specify whether or not to have SMS manage the Remote Assistance settings and whether the administrator should be able to override the Remote Assistance user settings.

The Security properties enable the administrator to identify permitted viewers, using the **Permitted Viewers** list. These viewers are users and user groups that are granted permission to remotely access site clients. The **Permitted Viewers** list applies to both SMS Remote Tools and Remote Assistance users; it defines who can remotely access clients in addition to members of the local Administrators group. Using SMS 2003, members of the local Administrators group can access clients, whether they appear in the Permitted Viewers list or not. To use Remote Tools on clients running Windows NT 4.0 or later requires that the user be a member of the local Administrators group or be included in the Permitted Viewers list.

Membership in the **Permitted Viewers** list must be coupled with the security right to use remote tools on specific collections. This security right is assigned to a user or user group. For more information about setting security permissions for collections refer to Chapter 4 of this document. Do not, however, rely solely on Remote Tools security rights in Collections to limit access to systems since Remote Tools can also be activated from the command line, in which case collection security rights are bypassed and only the **Permitted Viewers** list controls access. The **Permitted Viewers** list is always in effect, regardless of how Remote Tools is activated; hence, the **Permitted Viewers** list should always be used to limit access.

When entering a user identity into the **Permitted Viewers** list, be sure to use an identity of a valid domain user. SMS does not check to ensure that the user is a valid domain user and hence any error in entry would not be detected. Include the domain when specifying accounts in the **Permitted Viewers** list.

The Policy properties define the level of remote access and the administrator permission level. There are three levels of access that can be assigned to the Remote Tools user for access to a client: **Full**, **Limited**, and **None**. The default setting for access level is **Full**. The **Full** access level allows all remote functions and diagnostics to run. The **Limited** access level allows selected remote individual functions; these functions are described in Table 8 below and are not necessarily enabled by default. The settings button on the Policy properties page is used to view/set these individual functions. Remote control is prohibited by the **None** access level.

> NOTE: If the level of access is changed from Full to Limited, all the possible settings shown in Table 8 remain enabled by default. If, on the other hand, the access level is changed from None to Limited, none of the possible settings will be enabled by default.

The administrator permission level options (on the Policy properties tab) either require the Remote Tools user to ask for client user permission to run remote tools or allow the Remote Tools user to run the tools without asking for the client user's permission.

Table 8. Remote Tools Settings

Possible Settings for Remote Tools Usage
☑ View client screen and control its keyboard
☑ Run commands on client computer
☑ Transfer files to and from client computer
☑ Restart client computer
☑ Exchange text messages with client (chat)
☑ View client computer configuration

UNCLASSIFIED

Also included in the Policy properties is the level of access allowed for the Remote Assistance option. If Remote Assistance is used, the level of access can be set to **Full control**, **Remote viewing,** or **None**.

The Notification properties specify how a client will be notified when a Remote Tools session has been started. Both visual and audible indicators can be enabled but are not enabled by default on the client. Either or both of these indicators can be chosen by the administrator at the server as the means of notification to the client. If the administrator chooses no indicators, the client **will not** be notified when a Remote Tools session has been established.

The Advanced properties must be configured before enabling the client agent; changes to the Advanced properties made after enabling the client agent will not automatically be distributed to the client machines. Other than this exception, changes made to the client agent properties from the SMS Administrator Console are distributed to and implemented on all clients on a site-wide basis[14].

Client

The clients receive the Remote Tools software and configuration from the SMS Site Server. As described previously, the client agents are configured from the SMS Administrator Console and these configurations are distributed to the clients. When Remote Tools has been activated on a client, a Remote Control icon is available from the Control Panel of the client machine. Unless the SMS administrator denies users the ability to change their Notification and Policy tab settings for the client, users can open **Remote Control** in Control Panel and use the **Remote Control Properties** dialog box to change these settings. In particular, a user can specify the level of remote access that is allowed. If a user specifies **Full** or **None**, administrators can use all or none of the Remote Tools functions respectively on that user's client machine. If a user specifies **Limited** remote access, the user can restrict the administrator to using only the Remote Tools functions that the user specifies. For these reasons, do not allow clients to change these settings. You specify this in the site-wide settings.

Remote Assistance and Terminal Services

These features are available only for certain client configurations. The Remote Assistance capability is available when the SMS Administrator Console and the client are both running either Windows XP Professional or a Windows .NET Server. The Terminal Services feature is available when the client has the Terminal Services Client installed and enabled. Both Remote Assistance and Terminal Services are operating system options. Remote Assistance is briefly discussed later in this chapter.

Security

To securely configure and operate remote tools, the administrator must properly set collection security, viewer list security, and client permission security as well as taking other security measures.

If you create a specific Remote Tools administrator account, it must be given the security right to use remote tools on the specific collections containing the clients. This is done by setting **Collection Security Rights** from the properties menu (the **Security** tab of the collection properties window) for the selected collection. This account must also be granted access to the SMS console and the SMS files.

---

[14]   It is possible to force a redistribution of properties to the clients by disabling and reenabling the remote clients; see the SMS Administrator's Guide for details.

Be aware that collection security does not provide a fail-safe means of protecting the usage of remote tools. If remote tools are run using the Remote.exe program from the command line, collection security can be bypassed. Remote.exe enforces security the way that running Remote Tools from the SMS Administrator Console does. However, Remote.exe has a /SMS:nosql switch that does not enforce collection security. The /SMS:nosql switch allows one to use SMS Remote Tools even when the SMS site is unavailable.

The Remote Tools administrator or group must be listed in the **Permitted Viewers** list. These viewers are users and user groups that are granted permission to remotely access the site clients.

> NOTE: If a global group is a member of a local group and that local group is put on the Permitted Viewers list, members of the global group will not be enumerated by SMS and, therefore, will not be granted access permissions. To grant the access permissions to members of such a global group, explicitly specify the global group on the Permitted Viewers list.

The level of access to use remote tools can be set at the **Remote Tools Client Agent Properties.** The **Policy** tab selects the level of remote access allowed. The available levels are **Full**, **Limited**, and **None;** the settings involved in these levels are shown in Table 8. The access policy should be carefully reviewed if Remote Tools will be set at either **Full** or **Limited**. The access permission area can be set to enable the client to deny a request for a Remote Tools session. Enable the access permission for the client to deny a Remote Tools session request. For added protection against possible unauthorized use of Remote Tools, select the High-security visual indicator.

Remote Tools access can also be managed at the client level. The client agent can be enabled to not allow the client to change Remote Tools settings. On the Site Server, the **General** tab of the **Remote Tools Client Agent properties** has a checkbox that can be set so that the client cannot change the **Policy** or **Notification** settings. This checkbox is not enabled by default. As already recommended above, enable this checkbox to ensure that users cannot change Remote Tools settings.

Although access control for SMS Remote Tools can be implemented through the measures mentioned above, it does have limitations. The Remote Tools administrator user should always exercise caution. Due to the lack of a time-out function, the user should always exit from the Remote Tools window after using any remote tool functions on a specific object.

The remote execute function uses the security context of the administrator remotely executing the function. Therefore, any programs that are initiated using the remote execute function are run with the administrator's right, not the right of the user locally logged on to the client machine. This means that using the remote execute function could allow a user on the client computer to perform functions that they should not be allowed to do. Therefore, disable the remote execute capability. In the Remote Tools client agent properties window, select the Policy tab. In the SMS Remote Tools frame, change the **Level of remote access allowed** to Limited and click the Settings... button. In the Default Limited SMS Remote Tools Settings window, uncheck the **Run commands on client computer** checkbox. If you must run a command with administrative privilege, send it as a program in a package.

The Remote Tools user, using the Remote Tools Toolbox at the server to access the Remote Tools client agent on the client computer, should not enter passwords for privileged accounts on the client computer when using a remote control session. This would prevent the capture of passwords for the privileged accounts at the client through software that can observe the input.

UNCLASSIFIED

Remote Tools users should reboot the client computer if a Remote Tools session has failed while performing a remote function. This prevents leaving an open connection that does not time out.

Remote Assistance is available for Advanced Clients running Window XP, Windows Server 2003, or later. Although Remote Assistance is not a function of SMS, it can be accessed through the SMS Administrator Console. The Remote Assistance settings can be managed from the **General** tab of the **Remote Tools Client Agent Properties**. According to Microsoft, Windows Remote Assistance and Remote Desktop Connection, built-in features of the operating system, are more secure technologies than SMS Remote Control. [3, page 341] Select the option **Do not install Remote Control components for Advanced Clients running Window XP, Windows Server 2003, or later** to prevent Remote Control from being installed on computers running those operating systems. Use the Windows Remote Assistance and Remote Desktop Connection features of Windows XP and Windows Server 2003 rather than SMS Remote Control on computers running those operating systems.

The status of each site system is recorded in the Site System Status folder, which is contained in the System Status folder in the SMS Administrator Console. Remote Tools session activities can be viewed by performing a status message query for Remote Tools activities. These status messages are viewed through the SMS Status Message Viewer as discussed in Chapter 14 of this document. Check these status messages periodically to ensure that no unauthorized use of remote tools is occurring.

Important Security Points

- ❏ Always use the **Permitted Viewers** list to control access to Remote Tools.
- ❏ Include identification of the domain when specifying accounts in the **Permitted Viewers** list.
- ❏ Deny users the permission to change Remote Tools settings on their client machines.
- ❏ Set security rights on the collections containing the clients to give the Remote Tools administrator account access to use remote tools on those objects.
- ❏ Set the **Permitted Viewers** list to include only the Remote Tools administrator and users that have security rights on the collections containing the clients.
- ❏ Set the Remote Tools Policy to enable the client to deny a request for a Remote Tools session.
- ❏ Select the High-security visual indicator under the Notification properties.
- ❏ Carefully review site policies to determine whether client users should be allowed to change the Remote Tools Policies on the client machine.
- ❏ Exit from the Remote Tools window after using any remote tool functions on a specific object.
- ❏ Disable the remote execute capability.
- ❏ As a Remote Tools user, do not enter passwords for privileged accounts on the client computer when using a remote control session.
- ❏ As a Remote Tools user, reboot the client computer if a remote tool session has failed while performing a remote function.

❑ Select the option **Do not install Remote Control components for Advanced Clients running Window XP, Windows Server 2003, or later** on the **General** tab of the **Remote Tools Client Agent Properties** dialog box. Use the Windows Remote Assistance and Remote Desktop Connection features of Windows XP and Windows Server 2003 rather than SMS Remote Control on computers running those operating systems.

❑ Periodically review the status messages for Remote Tools sessions.

UNCLASSIFIED

Inventory Collection

SMS provides inventory collection to simplify site-wide administrative tasks, such as keeping track of number of computers, number of software copies, computer hardware configurations, and software inventory. Inventory collection is available for all hardware and software on a site-wide basis. All inventory information is stored in the central SMS database and is viewed for each client in the Resource Explorer.

This chapter discusses the basic principles of inventory collection and relevant security protections. Inventory information's integrity and confidentiality should be protected to reduce the risk of unauthorized modification and the risk of an intruder leveraging the information for attack purposes.

Overview

Secure use of inventory collection begins with a basic understanding of its usage and components. Inventory collection gathers hardware and software information from SMS site clients. The inventory collection function consists of SMS server-side software and client agent software, as depicted in Figure 9.

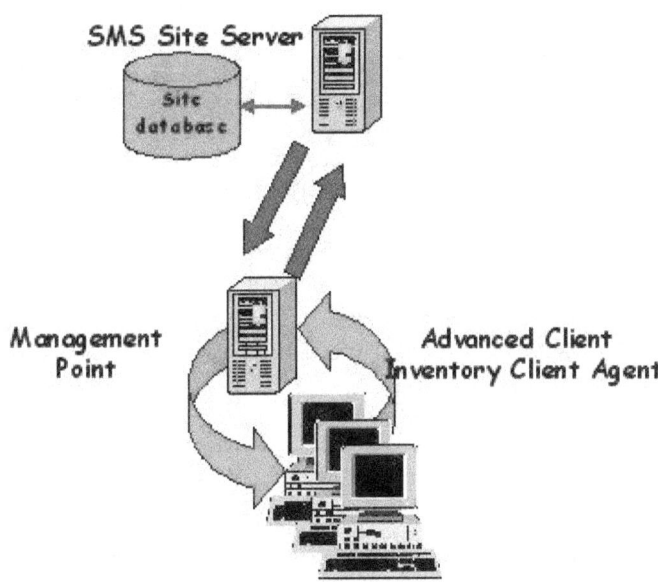

Figure 9. Hardware and Software Inventory

The client agent software gathers information about the hardware and the software for each client in the SMS site hierarchy. Advanced Clients use a single Inventory Client Agent. These client agents pass the inventory information to a Management Point. The

MPs provide communication points between the Site Server and the inventory client agents. The inventory information is received by the Management Point, which forwards it to the Site Server. The Site Server then stores the information in the SMS Site Database, making it available for generating and viewing reports.

> SOMETHING TO CONSIDER: The IDMIF and NOIDMIF collection can be used to extend SMS hardware inventory collection. Consider whether you should enable such collection in light of the security risk involved, as discussed in the SMS Concepts, Planning, and Deployment Guide. [1, page 191]

Installation and Configuration

Inventory Collection is installed as part of SMS. Also provided with the installation are the client agents needed on the client machines in order for Inventory Collection to operate.

Operation

Inventory collection is an unattended, scheduled process that collects hardware and software inventory information to aid other SMS administrative processes. When enabled, client agents collect the inventory data according to a predetermined schedule. The inventory data is sent to the MP and then sent on to the Site Server for processing and storage in the SMS Site Database.

Inventory data for individual clients can be viewed using the Resource Explorer tool. This tool enables an administrator to view hardware and software information about site clients. It is accessed by selecting an individual client in a collection and choosing the Start Resource Explorer menu item under the All tasks menu item. Read permission for the Collection object is needed to view the inventory data.

Security

SMS Inventory Collection has the auditing security feature built into it. Auditing provides a record of inventory agent installation and the inventory collection process. Log files on the client are enabled by default and are written automatically to the \MS\SMS\Logs folder. Log files should be reviewed when the Hardware Inventory process and/or the Software Inventory process is enabled. This should be done to determine that the client agent installation has been scheduled and that the installation has been successful. The inventory log files should also be reviewed periodically to ensure that the inventory processes are being completed successfully. SMS Trace provides the mechanism to view these log files.

> NOTE: SMS Trace is available in the Systems Management Server 2003 Toolkit 1, available for download at the Microsoft site—
> http://www.microsoft.com/smserver/downloads/2003/tools/toolkit.asp

Status messages should also be reviewed periodically to monitor client agent installation and the hardware/software inventory process.

Inventory data is passed from the client to the MP and stored there. This provides the opportunity for inadvertent disclosure of site hierarchy data. Data confidentiality should be protected by assigning NTFS permissions on the SMS_sitecode share for the MP server(s) and directory/files in accordance with the recommendations listed in Chapter 5

UNCLASSIFIED

of the *Systems Management Server Concepts, Planning, and Deployment Guide*. These settings should be verified occasionally.

In addition, do not collect client files as part of Software Inventory. If client file collection is required, be aware that sensitive files, such as system and client configuration files, could contain information that would be very useful to an adversary. These files could contain username and password combinations used during software installation, connection strings, details about the configuration of software installed on the client, and other, sensitive information. Determine appropriate protection mechanisms for these files before implementing client file collection.

Important Security Points

❏ Periodically use the SMS Trace to review hardware and software inventory log files.

❏ Monitor status messages to ensure proper inventory operation.

❏ Implement inventory data confidentiality and integrity by enforcing the recommended NTFS permissions on the shares, directories, and files of the MP server(s). [1, Chapter 5]

❏ Do not collect client files as part of Software Inventory. If absolutely necessary to collect client files, determine appropriate protection mechanisms for these files before implementing client file collection.

Queries and Reports

This chapter discusses queries and reports within SMS, focusing on the principle of least privilege in setting up accounts and permissions to use query and report features.

Queries

A query in SMS is a set of instructions that can extract information about objects in the SMS database using defined criteria. Queries can be run against any of the SMS objects, such as packages, software products, hardware, advertisements, users, and groups. However, queries do not span object types: that is, a query is always restricted to one type of object. SMS has a number of predefined queries. Users can modify these predefined queries or create new queries in the SMS Administrator Console. New *named queries* are stored in the SMS Site Database. These appear under **Queries** in the SMS Administrator Console. A named query searches the database for information about the objects that match the query criteria. SMS uses queries to populate collections and to provide the results for reports.

Queries constitute an object class in SMS and, as with other classes, permissions can be set so that only specified users or groups can access the queries. Permissions can be set at the class level—that is, for all queries—or for specific queries. When a query is created, the user creating the query gets Read, Modify, and Delete permissions to the query. Because a query must access objects to get its results, the user running the query must have permission to access the objects or the query will not execute. When a query is run, the results are displayed in the SMS Administrator Console results pane. In order to run a query, the user must have permissions to execute the SMS Administrator Console, to access the Queries folder, and to access the relevant data in the SMS database. In keeping with the principle of least privilege, restrict access to queries to those who need access to the data.

Reports

Reporting depends on one or more site systems being enabled as a Reporting Point. A *Reporting Point* is a site system that hosts the code for Report Viewer. In order to be a Reporting Point, the site system must have IIS 5.0 or later installed and enabled. In order to access a Reporting Point, a user must be a member of the SMS Reporting Users group on the Reporting Point. Administrators are automatically made a member of this group.

Reports can be created and managed using the SMS Administrator Console. Reports are run and displayed by Report Viewer, which requires Internet Explorer 5 or later. The results of a report can be viewed and the list of reports navigated in Report Viewer.

Report Viewer can be run from the SMS Administrator Console or can be run independently. Report Viewer can be started from the SMS Administrator Console by right-clicking a report, choosing a Reporting Point, and clicking **Run**. When using Report

UNCLASSIFIED

Viewer from the SMS Administrator Console, the specific Reporting Point to be used must be selected. Report Viewer can also be started by entering a report's unique URL in the **Address** box of Internet Explorer, or by entering the URL of the Report Viewer home page on a Reporting Point in the **Address** box of Internet Explorer.

A user must have **Create** permission for the Reports object class to create or import reports. A user must also have the appropriate permissions for the Reports object class or instance to modify, delete, export, or run a report. **Read** permission for particular report objects is sufficient access for most report users. With **Read** permission for a report, a user can view the name of the report in the reports list using either Report Viewer or the SMS Administrator Console, as appropriate, and can run the report using Report Viewer. SMS administrators may require additional permissions. Employ the principle of least privilege in assigning permissions for reports and the objects they report on.

Whether Report Viewer is used through the SMS Administrator Console or by non-administrative viewers who connect to Reporting Points, the user must be a member of the SMS Reporting Users group on the Reporting Point and must have **Read** permission on the requested report. Be careful when adding users to the Reporting Users group. As long as the group is granted access to execute the report, members of this group do not require SMS Object Security permissions on the objects being reported on. For example, a user with the security right to run a report of collections can list all collections, even if that user does not have collection permissions or is only granted permissions on certain collections. Limit this exposure by ensuring that the SQL statement used by the report limits the results to data that the user has been authorized to see.

Since reports provide information about the client computers across the SMS hierarchy and the current state of managed systems across an organization, regularly review reports as part of secure operations using SMS.

SQL Server Views

The principal element of a report is a SQL (Structured Query Language) statement that defines which data the report gathers and returns. The SQL statement in a report does not run directly against the SMS Site Database tables. Rather, the SQL statement runs against a set of SQL Server views, which point to records in the SMS Site Database tables. Each time a report is run, the information returned consists of data that is current in the database at that time. To create new reports by using the SMS Administrative Console requires a working knowledge of SQL.

To use Reporting, it is not necessary to configure access rights to the SQL Server views or tables in the SMS Site Database. SMS 2003 internally controls database access and security. To access the SQL Server views using an application other than SMS, it is necessary to create additional SQL Server users and configure database access rights. During setup, SMS 2003 configures a role named **smsschm_users** for the SMS Site Database and grants this role **Select** permission to all SQL Server views. To create additional SQL Server users who can access the SQL Server views, those users must be included in the **smsschm_users** database role membership using SQL Server. If access to SQL Server views is necessary, permission should be granted to access the SQL Server views only, not to access the SMS Site Database tables.

Supplemental Reports

Supplemental reports are reports created outside SMS 2003. Supplemental reports can be placed in a designated folder on a Reporting Point and can be displayed by Report Viewer to extend the reporting capabilities. Supplemental reports can be any files that can be displayed using Internet Explorer 5 or later. Supplemental reports are not secured

UNCLASSIFIED

SMS objects. Thus, if a supplemental report requires security protection, the steward of the report must provide the protection by some appropriate means since security of supplemental reports cannot be provided by SMS.

Links in Reports

Reports can contain links to additional information not contained in the report. A link can be to another report, to the Computer Details Page, or to the Status Message Details Page. The Computer Details Page and the Status Message Details Page are specialized pages used in Report Viewer to view reports dealing with information about computers and status messages. A link can also be a URL. In order to view the additional information referenced by the link, the user must have the appropriate permissions to the link target. For example, if a report links to the Status Message Details page, the user must have Read permission for the Status Message object to view status message details. If a report links to another report, the user must have instance-level Read permission for that report or the Report class-level Read permission to view the target report.

When creating links in reports, the proper security measures must be taken to ensure that information is not revealed to users who do not have the need or the authority to view it.

Important Security Points

❑ Restrict access to queries to those who need access to the data.

❑ Use the principle of least privilege in assigning permission on reports and the objects they report on. If reports are to be run by users who do not otherwise need administrator permissions, give **Read** permission to the specific instances of the reports they need, not to the class of all reports.

❑ Ensure that SQL statements used by reports limit their results to data that the user has been authorized to see.

❑ Regularly review reports.

❑ If access to SQL Server views is necessary, grant permission to access the SQL Server views only, not permission to access the SMS Site Database tables.

❑ If a supplemental report requires security protection, provide the protection by some appropriate means other than SMS, since SMS does not provide security for supplemental reports.

❑ When creating links in reports, take the proper security measures to ensure that information is not revealed to users who do not have the need or authority to view it.

Chapter

14

Status and Logs

Status messages, status summaries, and logs provide useful tools for troubleshooting SMS problems. This chapter gives a summary of these tools to provide a context for the security recommendations affecting their use.

Status Messages

SMS status messages are text messages generated by SMS component servers as they execute. Status messages are of two types: flow-of-activity messages, which illustrate the progress of a task within a component, and exceptional messages, which indicate that a problem has been encountered. All status messages are stored in the SMS database. Both servers and clients can generate status messages. Status messages can be viewed with the SMS Status Viewer, which is part of the SMS Administrator Console. The Status Viewer groups messages from similar functional areas.

Each status message is stamped with a severity—Error, Warning, or Informational. Status messages also have a type—Milestone, Detail, or Audit. Milestone messages indicate success or failure of an operation. Detail messages contain details of operations. Audit status messages provide an audit trail of actions taken in the SMS Administrator Console that added, modified, or deleted objects. Status messages are stamped with date and time, which can be configured to use Greenwich Mean Time if desired for geographically dispersed sites. Messages also contain Source, Site, System Name, Component Name, Message ID, Description, and other optional fields.

Status Viewer

The SMS Status Viewer displays status messages and status summaries for the user. SMS produces *status summaries,* from status messages and other data, for Components, Sites, Advertisements, and Packages. These summaries can include counts of status messages, other state information, or both. Summaries are based on *display intervals,* which can be specified by the user. Status messages can also be displayed based on display intervals.

Status summaries include color-coded indicators that reflect thresholds related to status messages. Critical, Warning, and OK are the three color-coded indicators, red, yellow, and green respectively. The administrator can define the thresholds to determine when status indicators are displayed. For example, a threshold could be set on how low the amount of free space can go or how many warning messages are required before a critical status indicator is displayed. These thresholds can be viewed with SMS Status Viewer.

To view SMS status information, it is necessary to have the **Read** SMS object security right to the sites and to status message objects. Restrict access to the status message object class to SMS administrators.

Status Configuration

SMS Administrator Console provides options for configuring the status system in the **Status Reporting Properties** dialog box under **Component Configuration.** Configuration options control which messages are reported, which messages are logged to the Windows Event Log, whether to report detail messages on failure, and message filtering rules. Message filtering rules determine when messages are processed and possibly discarded. There are options that control replication of messages to parent sites. There is also an option that determines whether to save a status message in the SMS database and whether to additionally save a status message in the event log.

The status system can also be configured to activate external user-defined programs. Status filter rules can trigger privileged programs as well as resource intensive programs. Therefore, the creation of rules should be limited to SMS administrators. The **Manage Status Filters** SMS site object class or instance right is necessary to create these rules. The Status summarizers can be turned off and status message deletion properties and rules can be set, such as the length of time a message should be retained. Configuration includes options on how to export messages as text files as well as some format choices.

Log Files

Configuration capability includes an option for components to create log files. This option is on by default on the Site Server in SMS2003. Component log files are enabled through the SMS Service Manager utility in the SMS Administrator Console. Log files are text files that are written to a default folder—the *SMS\Logs* folder—unless otherwise specified when logging is enabled. Log files can be viewed using any text editor or using SMS Trace. SMS Trace provides a real time display, whereas a text editor would display some static version of the file(s). Log files provide audit data for determining whether processes, such as inventory collection, are working properly. Logging is also intended for use as a troubleshooting and diagnostic tool, including investigation of security incidents. Lock down log files to protect their integrity.

See the Inventory Collection chapter for additional discussion of client log files.

Important Security Points

❑ Periodically review status messages related to SMS Administrator Console actions for unauthorized or suspicious activity.

❑ Restrict access to the status message object class to SMS administrators.

❑ Restrict the **Manage Status Filters** right for the site object class and instances to SMS administrators.

❑ Enable component log files on the Site Server.

❑ Use log files for security audits and, where appropriate, to investigate security incidents.

❑ Lock down log files.

UNCLASSIFIED

Summary

This guide has reviewed functional areas of Systems Management Server from a security perspective. The review generated important security points for administrators to consider.

This summary has two parts. Part 1 recaps the main features of SMS security. Part 2 summarizes the important security points that were made throughout the document.

Summary of Security Features

SMS defines and manages security rights mainly through accounts. A security right is a functional level of access given to a user[15]. It has three parts: a user or user group, a permission, and a security object. Individual user identities and group identities provide user identification; passwords provide authentication capability. SMS uses defined permissions to effect access control over SMS resources.

The management of security rights is the main security feature of SMS. In addition, SMS provides or uses auditing capabilities for many purposes.

SMS Accounts and Consoles

Advanced security mode is new in SMS 2003. This mode provides better security in its handling of accounts than does standard security mode. Advanced security mode does not require accounts other than the local System account and the computer account. It does not use the traditional *SMSService* account that is used in standard security mode. Local System and computer accounts are automatically maintained by the operating system. This ensures that no user knows their passwords and no manual maintenance is required.

The SMS Administrator Console is the primary interface for managing SMS features and tools and for administering an SMS hierarchy. It allows the maximum possible scope of access to an administrator. A custom console can restrict access to just those classes and instances that are necessary for an administrator's role. Good security practice suggests creating custom consoles for SMS administrators with restricted roles.

SMS Auditing

Log files for activities and events throughout the SMS operation can be enabled or created. Log files provide the means for auditing compliance with site policies, integrity of the objects managed by SMS, and availability of the services provided by SMS. Status messages, status summaries, and logs provide useful tools for troubleshooting SMS problems. The Status Message Viewer is a primary tool in this regard.

---

[15]   In SMS documentation, the security right is defined as a functional level of access given to an SMS Administrator. The discussion here extends the notion of a security right to users in general, although for the most part the security considerations pertain to SMS administrators.

UNCLASSIFIED

Specific auditing opportunities have been identified throughout this guide, including

- Enabling logging of the Software Metering Processor operations and periodically reviewing the log file

- Verifying the operation of the Software Metering Processor by periodically reviewing its status in the Site System Status folder of the SMS Administrator Console

- Reviewing the status of each site system, which is recorded in the Site System Status folder

- Auditing the status messages and log files that are generated throughout the inventory installation and collection process

Summary of Important Security Points

The important security points deal with secure ways to use, configure, arrange, or install SMS. Table 9 is a compendium of the points appearing throughout this guide.

UNCLASSIFIED

Table 9. Compendium of Important Security Points

Chapter	Important Security Points
2 Architectural Considerations	❑ Do not install other services that use the LocalSystem account on Site Servers and systems.
	❑ Apply the security guidance of the applicable NSA guides to the operating system (Windows Server 2000 or Windows Server 2003) used by the site's installation of SMS 2003 and the security guidance provided by Microsoft for Windows Server 2003 as appropriate. [9, 10]
	❑ Apply the security guidance of the NSA guide for IIS. [7] Also, check the guidance provided by Microsoft for securing IIS; see page 139 of the Concepts, Planning, and Deployment guide. [1]
	❑ Install SQL Server on the SMS primary Site Server and do not use it for any other application.
	❑ Assign a strong password for the SQL Server sa account even though integrated Windows authentication mode is used.
	❑ Use a low privileged domain user account as the SQL Server service account.
	❑ Use the SMS Integrated security option.
	❑ Apply the security recommendations of the NSA guide on SQL Server. [4]
	❑ Install the SMS Provider on the primary Site Server where SQL Server is also installed.
	❑ Carefully select any users to be added to the SMS Admins group and make sure that no unnecessary users are in the group.
	❑ Create the fewest sites required for your environment.
	❑ Enable secure key exchange.
	❑ Use Internet Protocol Security (IPSEC) to encrypt communications between site systems and the Site Server.
	❑ Use Windows Server 2003 and IIS 6.0. If you use Windows Server 2000, lock it down using the NSA security guide. [10]
	❑ Keep site system components that require IIS separate from other site system components. If possible, have a separate server for each SMS role that requires IIS. If not, combine roles requiring IIS on one or more servers and do not assign other roles to the server(s).

Chapter	Important Security Points
3 Primary Site Server Installation	❑ Use custom installation ❑ Ensure that unnecessary SMS functions are not installed. ❑ Do not install SMS on a domain controller. ❑ Select advanced security mode during installation of SMS. ❑ Apply the recommendations of the SMS 2.0 Security Guide if standard security mode is required at your site. ❑ Install secondary Site Servers locally. ❑ Operate secondary Site Servers in advanced security mode. ❑ Under the Registry key **HKEY_LOCAL_MACHINE\SOFTWARE\Microsoft**, remove the **Power Users** group from the **SMS** key and all its subkeys. If the Power Users group must be retained for some operational reason, reduce its permissions on this **SMS** and its subkeys to **Read** permission only. ❑ Replace the **Everyone** group with the **Authenticated Users** group on the Registry key **HKEY_LOCAL_MACHINE\SOFTWARE\Microsoft\SMS\Client\Client Components\Remote Control\User Settings**, retaining **Full control**.
4 Collections	❑ Delete any default collections that will not be used, ❑ When roles are assigned for controlling instances of the Collections class, remove the unneeded default permissions that have been assigned by SMS. ❑ Use class and instance security permissions to maintain access restrictions on collections, applying the principle of least privilege in assigning the permissions. ❑ Take special care to ensure proper control over collections with respect to the possible interactions affecting resource privileges. ❑ Verify the membership in collections before using the collections with SMS functions such as software distribution.
5 Objects, Permissions, and Accounts	❑ Limit areas where both class and instance permissions are assigned. ❑ Verify that the least restrictive settings, based on class and instance reconciliation, are acceptable for each security right. ❑ Check that SMS administrators can manipulate only sites, packages, advertisements, and other SMS objects that they are authorized to manipulate. ❑ Inspect the SMS class and instance security permissions with the SMS Administrator Console and further restrict access to specific roles, applying the principle of least privilege.

UNCLASSIFIED

Chapter	Important Security Points
6 SMS Administrator Console	❑ Consider creating custom consoles on workstations for users other than the user of the SMS Administrator Console on the Site Server, giving them access only to those functions and objects that are necessary to their roles. ❑ Physically secure any machine running SMS Administrator Console. ❑ If the machine running the SMS Administrator Console cannot be physically secured, secure SMS Administrator Console sessions with a password-protected screen saver.
7 SMS Client Discovery	❑ Use SMS network discovery if there is risk of unauthorized computers or other devices being attached to the network. ❑ Do not disable SMS Heartbeat Discovery, which is enabled by default. ❑ Crosscheck the information collected by the different discovery methods. ❑ Verify that the machines discovered are only those that should be on the network.
8 SMS Client Installation	❑ Install Advanced Client in preference to Legacy Client wherever feasible in your site hierarchy. ❑ Do not install SMS Clients on domain controllers. ❑ When using Client Push Installation, specify the option to use local administrator accounts for installation on the clients. ❑ If Group Policy Software Installation is used, Use a hidden folder for a software distribution point to prevent users from browsing contents of the share point. ❑ Replace the **Everyone** group with the **Authenticated Users** group in the permissions on the client installation shares—SMS_sitecode share and SMS Client share. Reduce the permissions of this group to **Read** only.
9 Software Distribution	❑ Limit access to the primary Site Server to those who are trusted and need to have access to it. Give special attention to the security rights and object permissions at the central site and take necessary precautions to protect the associated SQL server database. ❑ Use the download method for package installation. ❑ Remove the **Everyone** group and add the **Authenticated Users** group for the Distribution Point package share. Grant the **Authenticated Users** group read access to the share. ❑ If not all users require access to a package, modify the access permissions to specify the least permissions required. ❑ Define package access accounts. ❑ Limit access for Management Point advertisements to the SMS accounts involved in distribution and to a restricted number of administrators.

Chapter	Important Security Points
	❑ Limit access to the Client Agent's folder on the SMS Administrator Console to those authorized to turn on or turn off software distribution for the site.
	❑ Protect locations where source files are stored, whether in compressed or uncompressed form.
	❑ Require an authentication means for source files, such as publisher certificates, digital signature, or hash value checking.
	❑ Put the source files on a machine or share used only by SMS or on a machine or share where only SMS and a select few administrators have access.
	❑ Review and test the software that will be offered for distribution and test the SMS packages that will be advertised.
	❑ When creating packages, turn on the checkbox **Disconnect users from Distribution Points**.
	❑ When creating a program for a package, select the option to **Run with user rights** unless the package requires administrative rights.
	❑ If administrative rights are needed for running a package's program, use the option to install **Only when no user is logged on**.
	❑ Avoid running a package program with administrative rights when a user is logged in and can interact with the program.
	❑ Once a package has been installed, delete it from the download cache.
	❑ Limit the number of administrators who can create new collections of targets.
	❑ Limit security permissions for modifying and creating advertisements.
	❑ When available, use Windows policies on *Software Restrictions* to allow clients to check installs against certificates.
	❑ Provide security protection for client machines to protect the integrity of the download cache.
	❑ Test modified packages before distributing them.
	❑ Use a Virtual Private Network to mitigate the possibility of a man-in-the-middle attack on a client connecting remotely.
	❑ Allow only trusted individuals to create, transport, and distribute material created by the Courier Sender process and ensure that they use a procedure that enables them to maintain control of the media and its contents.
	❑ Remove old software from the system; do not just disable its advertisement.
	❑ Partition the software distribution process into roles, each role having only the permissions required for the assigned portion of the process.

UNCLASSIFIED

Chapter	Important Security Points
	♦ Give the software-acquisition role Administer permission for the source file location and no other permissions associated with SMS.
	♦ Give the package-definition role Administer permission for packages; give everyone else only **Read** permission.
	♦ Give the package-distribution role the permissions necessary to effect distribution to a selection of users and computers and to monitor distribution progress but not rights to create new SMS packages or to modify old packages.
10 Software Metering	❑ Give the account that does Software Metering the Software Metering rule object security right and the Meter instance right.
	❑ Make permissions for Software Metering folders and files as restrictive as possible, default is System and local administrators group.
	❑ Take care to ensure that the named executable and version information are correct when specifying executable programs in Software Metering rules.
	❑ Assign a strong password to the Software Metering administrator account.
	❑ Periodically review the status information of the Software Metering Processor to discover error messages.
	❑ Enable logging of the Software Metering Processor.
	❑ Periodically review the log file for the Software Metering Processor.
	❑ Periodically review the Software Metering rules, configurations, and lists against site policy by running reports of Software Metering or running customized metering reports.

Chapter	Important Security Points
11 Remote Tools	❑ Always use the **Permitted Viewers** list to control access to Remote Tools. ❑ Include identification of the domain when specifying accounts in the **Permitted Viewers** list. ❑ Deny users the permission to change Remote Tools settings on their client machines. ❑ Set security rights on the collections containing the clients to give the Remote Tools administrator account access to use remote tools on those objects. ❑ Set the **Permitted Viewers** list to include only the Remote Tools administrator and users that have security rights on the collections containing the clients. ❑ Set the Remote Tools Policy to enable the client to deny a request for a Remote Tools session. ❑ Select the High-security visual indicator under the Notification properties. ❑ Carefully review site policies to determine whether client users should be allowed to change the Remote Tools Policies on the client machine. ❑ Exit from the Remote Tools window after using any remote tool functions on a specific object. ❑ Disable the remote execute capability. ❑ As a Remote Tools user, do not enter passwords for privileged accounts on the client computer when using a remote control session. ❑ As a Remote Tools user, reboot the client computer if a remote tool session has failed while performing a remote function. ❑ Select the option **Do not install Remote Control components for Advanced Clients running Window XP, Windows Server 2003, or later** on the **General** tab of the **Remote Tools Client Agent Properties** dialog box. Use the Windows Remote Assistance and Remote Desktop Connection features of Windows XP and Windows Server 2003 rather than SMS Remote Control on computers running those operating systems. ❑ Periodically review the status messages for Remote Tools sessions.

UNCLASSIFIED

Chapter	Important Security Points
12 Inventory Collection	❑ Periodically use the SMS Trace to review hardware and software inventory log files. ❑ Monitor status messages to ensure proper inventory operation. ❑ Implement inventory data confidentiality and integrity by enforcing the recommended NTFS permissions on the shares, directories, and files of the MP servers. [1, Chapter 5] ❑ Do not collect client files as part of Software Inventory. If absolutely necessary to collect client files, determine appropriate protection mechanisms for these files before implementing client file collection.
13 Queries and Reports	❑ Restrict access to queries to those who need access to the data. ❑ Use the principle of least privilege in assigning permission on reports and the objects they report on. If reports are to be run by users who do not otherwise need administrator permissions, give **Read** permission to the specific instances of the reports they need, not to the class of all reports. ❑ Ensure that SQL statements used by reports limit their results to data that the authorized users should be able to see. ❑ Regularly review reports. ❑ If access to SQL Server views is necessary, grant permission to access the SQL Server views only, not permission to access the SMS Site Database tables. ❑ If a supplemental report requires security protection, provide the protection by some appropriate means other than SMS since SMS does not provide security for supplemental reports. ❑ When creating links in reports, take the proper security measures to ensure that information is not revealed to users who do not have the need or authority to view it.
14 Status and Logs	❑ Periodically review status messages related to SMS Administrator Console actions for unauthorized or suspicious activity. ❑ Restrict access to the status message object class to SMS administrators. ❑ Restrict the **Manage Status Filters** right for the site object class and instances to SMS administrators. ❑ Enable component log files on the Site Server. ❑ Use log files for security audits and, where appropriate, to investigate security incidents. ❑ Lock down log files.

Appendix

A

References

1. Microsoft Corporation, October 2003, *The SMS 2003 Concepts, Planning and Deployment Guide*, Document No. X09-75009, Microsoft Corporation, One Microsoft Way, Redmond, WA 98052-6399.

2. Microsoft Corporation, ©1994-1999, *Systems Management Server Administrator's Guide*, on-line Help system, Microsoft Corporation, One Microsoft Way, Redmond, WA 98052-6399.

3. Microsoft Corporation, October 2003, *Operations Guide: Microsoft Systems Management Server, Version 2003*, Report Number X09-75018, Microsoft Corporation, One Microsoft Way, Redmond, WA 98052-6399.

4. Christman, S. M. and J. Hayes, Maj USAF, August 26, 2003, *Guide to the Secure Configuration and Administration of Microsoft SQL Server 2000*, Version 1.5, Network Applications Team of the Systems and Network Attack Center, National Security Agency, Ft. Meade, Maryland.

5. Haney, Julie N., September 13, 2001, *Guide to Securing Microsoft Windows 2000 Group Policy*, Version 1.1, Network Security Evaluations and Tools Division of the Systems and Network Attack Center, National Security Agency, Ft. Meade, Maryland.

6. Defense Information Systems Agency, Systems Management Server 2.0 Security Guide, STIG at https://iase.disa.mil/techguid/stig/index.html.

7. Walker IV, W. E. and S. M. Christman, October 29, 2003, *Guide to the Secure Configuration and Administration of Microsoft Internet Information Services 5.0*, Report Number C4-057R-00, Network Applications Team of the Systems and Network Attack Center (SNAC), National Security Agency, Ft. Meade, Maryland.

8. Microsoft, SMS 2003 SDK, HTML Help file, available for download at the Microsoft web site (www.microsoft.com).

9. Microsoft Solutions for Security Group, April 24, 2003, Windows Server 2003 Security Guide, Microsoft Corporation, One Microsoft Way, Redmond, WA 98052-6399.

10. NSA Web Site, http://www.nsa.gov/snac/downloads_win2000.cfm?MenuID=scg10.3.1.1

11. Microsoft Corporation, September 2004, *Scenarios and Procedures for Microsoft Systems Management Server 2003: Security*, Microsoft Corporation, One Microsoft Way, Redmond, WA 98052-6399.

12. Systems and Network Attack Center, July 12, 2002, *The 60 Minute Network Security Guide: (First Steps Towards a Secure Network Environment)*, Version 1.2, National Security Agency, 9800 Savage Rd., Suite 6704, Ft. Meade, MD.

Glossary

This appendix provides expansions for acronyms and definitions for technical terms used In this guide.

Acronyms

BITS	Background Intelligent Transfer Service
CAP	Client Access Point
IIS	Internet Information Services
IPSEC	Internet Protocol Security
IT	Information Technology
MMC	Microsoft Management Console
MOM	Microsoft Operations Manager
MP	Management Point
SMS	Systems Management Server 2003
SQL	Structured Query Language
URL	Uniform Resource Locator
WBEM	Web-based Enterprise Management
WMI	Windows Management Instrumentation

Definitions

Client Access Point: *See* SMS Client Access Point.

Client: *See* SMS Client.

Client Agent: A client agent is a computer program that runs on an SMS Client to perform the client side of an SMS function, such as inventory collection.

Component Server: A site system role that is filled by any SMS site system running an SMS component installed by SMS Site Component Manager. The only site system that is not a component server is the Distribution Point. See also SMS Site Server; SMS site system; SMS site system role.

Database: *See* SMS Site Database.

Distribution Point: *See* SMS Distribution Point.

Internet Information Services: Internet Information Service (IIS) is a web server used to publish and distribute web-based content to standard browsers and other systems, providing services such as WWW, FTP, and SMTP. It is used by SMS to support the Management Point, Server Locator Point, and Reporting Point site systems.

Management Point: *See* SMS Management Point.

Permission: Permissions are rules associated with a shared resource on a network or computer, such as a file, directory, or printer; permissions can be assigned to groups, and individual users.

Reporting Point: *See* SMS Reporting Point.

Security Right: A security right is a functional level of access given to a user[16]. A security right has three parts: a user or user group, a permission, and a security object. Thus, the management of security rights is seen to be a principal security feature of SMS 2003.

Server Locator Point: *See* SMS Server Locator Point.

Share: A share is a folder or a drive (a hard drive or portion thereof) that has been identified to the Windows operating system as a resource that can be shared with remote computers. The type of sharing (Read, Write, and so on) for a particular user or group is determined by the permissions that are associated with the share when it is defined.

Site Database: *See* SMS Site Database.

Site Hierarchy: *See* SMS Site Hierarchy.

Site Server: *See* SMS Site Server.

Site System Role: *See* SMS Site System Role.

Site System: *See* SMS Site System.

Site: *See* SMS Site.

SMS Administrator Console: The SMS Administrator Console is the primary interface used to configure, run, and access SMS features and tools, and to accomplish day-to-day tasks required to administer an SMS system. The SMS Administrator Console supports SMS sites configuration, SMS Site Database maintenance, and SMS hierarchy status monitoring.

SMS Administrator: An SMS administrator is a person responsible to configure, run, and use SMS tools to accomplish day-to-day tasks required to administer an SMS system. The SMS 2003 Administrator console is the primary interface used by an SMS administrator.

SMS Advanced Client: The SMS Advanced Client is the new client-agent package in SMS 2003. It includes all client agents needed to support SMS 2003 functions that are provided in the SMS Legacy Client, such as software distribution and inventory collection. In addition, it is optimized for mobile and remote clients and low-bandwidth connections and uses the local system security context and the computer account on the client to carry out SMS tasks, making it more secure than the SMS Legacy Client.

SMS Central Site: The SMS central site is the primary site at the top of the SMS hierarchy—not a child to any other site. The SMS Site Database at the central site acquires aggregate inventory and Software Metering data from the SMS hierarchy. At

---

[16] In SMS documentation, the security right is defined as a functional level of access given to an SMS Administrator. The definition here extends the notion of a security right to users in general, although for the most part the security considerations pertain to SMS administrators.

UNCLASSIFIED

the central site, an SMS Administrator can view and manage all sites and computers in the SMS hierarchy.

SMS Client Access Point: A site system with the Client Access Point (CAP) role provides a communication point between the SMS Site Server and Legacy Client computers. Computers contact CAPs to install and update SMS Legacy Client software. After SMS Legacy Client software has been installed on computers in a site, they contact a CAP for updated information from the SMS Site Server. Clients deliver collected files, inventory information, discovery data records, Software Metering data, and status information to CAPs.

SMS Client: An SMS client is any computer that is supported by SMS, has been assigned to an SMS site, and has SMS Client software installed.

SMS Distribution Point: An SMS Distribution Point is any server that stores the package files, programs, and scripts necessary for a package to execute successfully at an SMS client computer. A Distribution Point offers distribution packages either on a windows share or via the Background Intelligent Transfer Service (BITS) protocol.

SMS Management Point: An SMS site system having the Management Point (MP) role functions as the communication point between SMS Advanced Clients and the SMS Site Server. An MP has advertisements for packages and sends these to clients specified in a target collection.

SMS Primary Site: An SMS primary site is an SMS site that stores SMS data for itself and all the sites beneath in a SQL Server database, which is called the SMS Site Database. Primary sites have administrative tools, such as the SMS Administrator Console, that enable the SMS Administrator to directly manage the site. SMS Setup creates each primary site as a stand-alone site. Primary sites can have multiple secondary sites, all of which propagate data to the primary site.

SMS Reporting Point: An SMS site system having the SMS Reporting Point role hosts the code for the SMS Report Viewer and any supplemental reports.

SMS Secondary Site: An SMS secondary site is an SMS site that does not have an SMS Site Database. It is attached to and reports to a primary site. A secondary site is managed by an SMS Administrator running an SMS Administrator Console connected to the primary site. A secondary site forwards the information it has gathered from SMS clients, such as computer inventory data and SMS system status information, to its parent site. The primary site then stores the data of both itself and the secondary site in the SMS Site Database.

SMS Server Locator Point: A Server Locator Point is an SMS site system that locates CAPs and MPs for SMS clients.

SMS Site Database: The SMS Site Database is a SQL Server database at an SMS primary site that stores SMS data for itself and all the sites beneath it in the site hierarchy.

SMS Site Hierarchy: An SMS site hierarchy is a set of SMS sites related to each other in such a way as to abstractly form a tree structure. An SMS site hierarchy resembles an organizational flowchart and exists whenever two or more SMS sites have been defined in a parent-child relationship. In general, management and configuration data moves down the hierarchy from higher level sites (from root of tree toward leaves). Resource and client data move up the hierarchy from lower level sites. More specifically, a parent site sends management instructions and data intended for client distribution down to its child sites. Child sites report their status up to their parent sites. This status includes the information it has gathered from SMS clients, such as computer inventory data, and SMS system status information.

SMS Site Server: The SMS Site Server is the Windows server on which SMS has been installed.

SMS Site System Role: Site systems are computers running supported Windows server operating systems or server shares that provide Systems Management Server (SMS) functionality to your site. Each site system plays one or more roles in supporting an SMS site. Some site system roles can be assigned to site systems within the site by configuring the site system, while others are automatically assigned by the system.

SMS Site System: An SMS site system is a Windows server that performs one or more SMS roles for an SMS site. The possible roles are Management Point, Server Locator Point, Reporting Point, Client Access Point, Distribution Point, and Software Metering server.

SMS Site: The SMS Site is the fundamental administrative unit in SMS. It defines the computers, users, groups, and other resources managed by SMS. An SMS site is bounded by a group of subnets that are defined by the SMS Administrator using IP subnets and/or Active Directory site names. This means that SMS can manage computers based on their subnet addresses or Active Directory site membership.

SMS Software Metering Server: An SMS Software Metering server is an SMS site system that supports monitoring of software running on computers within the SMS site to detect and report use of computer programs within the SMS site.

SMS Legacy Client: The SMS Legacy Client is a client-agent package containing the client agents needed to carry out SMS functions at an SMS Client, such as software distribution and inventory collection. The SMS Legacy Client in SMS 2003 is based on the SMS 2.0 Client; thus, it relies heavily on domain accounts to carry out key tasks on the SMS client computer. (Compare to SMS Advanced Client.)

Software Metering Server: *See* SMS Software Metering Server.

SQL Server: SQL Server is a relational database server that can be installed on a Microsoft Windows (NT or later) system. SMS uses SQL Server for storing and accessing the SMS site database.

UNCLASSIFIED

www.ingramcontent.com/pod-product-compliance
Lightning Source LLC
Chambersburg PA
CBHW080311290526
45790CB00005B/1993